Keys to Racing Success

KEYS TO

DODD, MEAD & COMPANY
NEW YORK

RACING

SUCCESS

By Bob Bavier

Design by Stanley S. Drate

1 2 3 4 5 6 7 8 9 10

Library of Congress Cataloging in Publication Data

Bavier, Robert Newton, 1918-
  Keys to racing success.

  1. Sailboat racing. 2. Yacht racing.
I. Title
GV826.5.B36   797.1′4   82-2358
ISBN 0-396-08064-2   AACR2

Contents

Preface
by Paul Elvström

HENRIK HANSEN

The Danish sailor Paul Elvström, over a period extending from 1948 to 1974, amassed a racing record that will in all likelihood never be equaled. He won four Olympic gold medals, sailing a Firefly in 1948 and Finns in 1952, 1956, and 1960. He won twelve world championships in eight different classes: 505 in 1957 and 1958, Finn in 1958 and 1959, Snipe in 1959, Flying Dutchman in 1962, 5.5 in 1966, Star in 1966 and 1967, Soling in 1969 and 1974, and Half-Ton in 1971.

Keys to Racing Success is such a good book that it is an honor for me to write a preface. This book has only one fault, namely that I did not write it myself!

As I read through the various chapters I kept reliving experiences in my own sailing career. I remembered when I had won by being bold, by jibing on the lifts, by anticipating, by being objective. I relived the hours spent in preparing and in practicing. I could recollect so many times when I had done well by sailing low on a reach and sweeping into the lead late in the leg.

And, yes, I can and do remember the occasions when I lost out by not following the precepts that Bob espouses, by being a sheep, for example, or by hesitating over the interpretation of a right-of-way rule and in consequence losing a commanding position.

The chapter on the importance of competing against the best is so very true. If I had not sailed against world-class sailors I could not possibly have become one.

Keys to Racing Success, however, will help sailors at all levels—the beginner, the good sailor, and the expert. It will help them because it focuses on what *really* makes the difference between winning and losing, between doing poorly or moving up in the fleet. The expert sailor may well know all that is recommended here, but even for the very best there is so much of value here to remind him of the essentials of a winning performance and to make him aware of the vital importance of certain keys.

Bob's lively way of reporting from his many years of experience on the race course both with and against keen sailors makes learning from him a pleasure. His great sense of humor makes this book most engrossing.

The final chapter in which Bob emphasizes the importance of having fun if you hope to do well hit home to me in particular. For many years I was fortunate in being able to do well in a variety of classes and events and I enjoyed myself immensely in the process. There then came a period when the burden of continuing to win became too much for me. I came close to suffering a nervous breakdown and my racing suffered. But two years later I became okay again, and sailed again for fun, and it was wonderful again. Wonderful too was the fact that I was able to regain my form and win the 1974 Soling Worlds for the second time (my first world championship in several years). I couldn't possibly have come back that way if I had not first recaptured the joy of racing, win or lose.

By absorbing what *Keys to Racing Success* has to say, sailors at every level are sure to improve. In my opinion, this is the best book yet that Bob has sent to the printers.

Foreword
by Buddy Melges

Buddy Melges is considered by many people (including Bob Bavier) to be the best sailor in the world today. His victories include two Star World Championships in 1978 and 1979; bronze and gold Olympic medals in Flying Dutchman 1964 and Soling 1972; Mallory Cup 1959, 1960, and 1961; thirteen I.L.Y.A. Scow Championships from 1949 to 1981; and the Nite Iceboat Worlds 1979 and 1981. In 1961, 1972, and 1978 he was voted "Yachtsman of the Year" and in 1972 was awarded the Nathanael G. Herreshoff Trophy for the most outstanding contribution to the sport of sailing in North America.

In *Keys to Racing Success* Bob Bavier translates the experiences he and others have had into information that sailors on every level will find useful. Bob has been an active and successful sailor for many years and during that time has contributed a great deal to the sport. His new book adds to the store of information he has shared with us to date by identifying and analyzing those elements that can spell the difference between victory and defeat on the race course—those basic "keys" that we all should focus on and use. Follow his advice and you'll be pleased with the results.

I read *Keys to Racing Success* just before competing in Florida in the 1981 S.O.R.C.'s Lipton Cup and then in a Star Class regatta. As I studied each chapter I found myself reliving every one of the situations he discusses. Out on the race course, I found his message ringing true time and time again.

Take the downwind leg, for example. Too few sailors recognize the fact that the wind shifts just as much on the run as on the beat. Often the skipper who is in phase with the shifts going upwind stops thinking when he rounds the mark and his downwind performance shows it. There's no excuse for that now, though. Bob's chapter "Jibe on the Lifts" says it straight, and my last race in that Star Series was a case in point. As we began the final run, I was in fourth place and needed a first to take the series. I felt a veer from the left, checked the telltales and compass, and checked the fleet. I elected to hold my enemies for a few moments on the starboard jibe, then jibed into the veer first and charged by three boats to win big.

"Don't Cover Early—Do Cover Late" is another Bavier axiom that too many sailors fail to understand and use. How many times have you been covered in the first five minutes of a race? Look up, and you'll probably see the new kid on the block fresh from being confused over some book on defensive sailing. Covering early in a race is death, except in a few cases, and Bob's comments on the subject tell you how the sailing game should be played both offensively and defensively.

His advice in the chapter "Don't Be a Sheep" deserves careful study, too. There's a time and a place for every tactic and a sheep will never win a safe leeward, a mark rounding, a protest, or a race. Well done, Bob.

What's my advice? Put yourself in the boat with Bob as he takes you from the dock to the starting line, around the course, and back to the dock. Know the rules, know Bob's rules, and you'll be a better sailor for it.

Introduction

When I completed the manuscript for this book I screwed up my courage and asked the two small-boat sailors whom I consider the best in the world over the last several decades if they would write forewords. The one condition was that they do it only if they really liked the book and really felt it made a new contribution to success on the race course. So the fact that Paul Elvström and Buddy Melges agreed readily and wrote such glowing forewords is flattering and gratifying to me. Far more important is the fact that they feel the book will help sailors at all levels. It makes me feel the effort was worthwhile. An author always hopes his book will sell well, but he also hopes it will help the reader achieve his goals and be glad he bought it. I'm now beginning to believe that *Keys to Racing Success* will succeed in that respect.

I want to also thank in particular two people who are keen sailors but hardly at the world-class level. My daughter, Louise, did far more than type the manuscript. She criticized sections that she thought were obscure or stuffy, and the changes I made as a result are, I believe, an improvement. Thanks also to Mark Smith, who did the illustrations. Mark is far more than a good illustrator. He is a fine sailor and made some sound suggestions for improvement in the text. It was a joy to work with an artist who could follow my crude sketches and translate them into something accurate and easy to visualize. He often suggested illustrations (both his own drawings and photographs) that he thought would add to the reader's understanding and I invariably went along with everything he proposed. The fact that both Louise and Mark are also keen for the book strengthens my hope that it will indeed be helpful to racing sailors at all levels of ability.

Thanks also to the photographers who spent so many hours combing through their files to dredge up appropriate pictures. It is never easy to find the right photograph. You know it exists, but only hard digging will unearth it. These photographers refused to give up and the results show it.

In *Keys to Racing Success* I'd like to share with you my personal excitement about this sport, and I hope that the book will give you more success and more enjoyment on the race course.

BOB BAVIER

Keys to Racing Success

1

DISCOVERING THE KEYS

*T*here are thousands of good sailors in this country and many other thousands around the world who do well in racing but are not consistent winners. There are an even greater number of smart, dedicated, experienced, and well-coordinated men and women who have raced for many years, read a number of books and articles on the sport, and who still keep finishing in the middle of the fleet. Sometimes they might get to the top third, but in high-level competition they never progress further. This phenomenon applies not only to world-class races but also to local club races, in which the same sailors win year after year.

Why is this? Why, with so many experienced sailors, do just a few get to the top, and why do those few manage to stay there when so many are trying to knock them off? Why, for example, has Paul Elvström won four Olympic gold medals and twelve world championships? Why, over the past twenty years, has Buddy Melges excelled in every class he has sailed? What makes Dennis Conner win? How, after years of just average sailing, did

Ted Turner fight his way to the top in both ocean and closed-course racing? Why is it that year after year, when it comes time to select the yachtsman and yachtswoman of the year, the same people are in contention for the award, with only an occasional newcomer? Buddy Melges, for example, has won the award three times, the first one in 1961 and the last one in 1978. When he didn't win, he was always one of the nominees and often in the top five (fourth, for example, in 1979). Ted Turner's reign has been shorter, but he has now won it four times (1970, 1973, 1977, and 1979).

One could conclude that the very complexity of yacht racing makes it impossible for all but a select few to excel. I simply will not buy that, even though it is true that in many respects yacht racing is the most complicated of sports. Other sports have set playing fields, which not only do not move but which also have precise dimensions. All sailing courses are of different lengths and different configurations, and, especially in tidal waters, the "field" is moving. If the wind held steady in both direction and velocity throughout the race, and if there were no currents, it would be a far less complicated sport. But, of course, the wind is never steady, and it is always changing, shifting more in certain parts of the race course than in others. Certain other sports are somewhat affected by wind (ask a golfer or football place kicker), but the effect is relatively minor and the same for all competitors. In sailing, the wind and its vagaries are all important. More important still is the need to forecast future wind directions and velocities.

The very complexity of sailing, the fact that there are so many variables and that conditions are never identical from race to race, gives yacht racing a special appeal. It is not enough to be able to "run" faster than your opponents. You also have to pick the most favorable spot to run in, to forecast the changes in variables, and thus be able to take advantage of them.

There is some truth to the saying that "watching a yacht race is as exciting as watching grass grow," but there is nothing boring for the participants. Using their minds and senses even more than their brawn, coordination, agility, and feel, they have to be constantly alert to changing situations.

Despite yacht racing's complexity, the tactics and techniques of winning are well known to thousands. There are a number of books in which the experts tell all they know about what it takes to win. I wrote one myself in 1947 entitled *Sailing to Win* in which I presented in considerable detail what I knew about how to win. Over the years it has been updated several times. Every month the leading yachting magazines present articles by expert sailors. If you ask top sailors for pointers on how to win, most of them will be only too willing to give advice.

In short, thousands of sailors appear to know the intricacies of the sport well enough and have enough natural ability to win either on a club, national, or world level. Still, the same people keep winning year after year. Why? For a long time I couldn't come up with an answer. Because the question intrigued me, I was determined to find out.

I felt fortunate in having the varied experience that might lead to an answer. My dad was an outstanding sailor, and by analyzing some of what I learned from him, I thought I could find some of the keys. I decided to analyze the successes and failures I had experienced in a lifetime of sailing, plus the successes and failures of the greatest sailors I have had the pleasure of sailing with and against. I also thought of the world-class sailors I had watched as a judge in several Olympic regattas, as a member of the Selection Committee for the America's Cup, and as a yachting writer covering major events. In a lifetime of sailing, I've skippered everything from dinghies to ocean racers and America's Cup defenders, sometimes with success, sometimes without. I've sailed with and against such greats as Bill Cox, Ted Hood, Briggs Cunningham, Ted Turner, Dennis Conner, Bob Derecktor, and other stars. I've raced over a period of years against the likes of Artie Knapp, Cornie Shields, George Hinman, and Bus Mosbacher. As a young man I competed in the International One Design Class during its heyday, and did frostbiting at Larchmont in its prime era. I've raced for the Admiral's Cup, sailed against the best in the Lightning Class and in Solings, and logged many thousands of miles of ocean racing both in the United States and abroad.

I cite all of this only to illustrate my experience as a sailor and as an observer of world-class sailors in action, experience upon which I have relied to discover what it is that separates the winners from the average competitors.

It took me a while to find the answer, but at long last I believe I've got it. *There are certain keys to success that the winners observe,* sometimes knowingly but often unwittingly. Some are so simple that they seem almost too easy a solution and are often overlooked. But I'm confident that, if observed, they will enable sailors of all abilities to do better, perhaps dramatically better. These keys to success will help only if you believe in their vital importance and have the discipline to practice them. In an effort to convince the reader, I'll illustrate each key with an anecdote or a reference to an expert sailor who wins by observing it.

If you are a beginner who is aiming high, this book in itself won't make you a winner. You've got to read other books and articles to develop a full understanding of the sport. You've got to compete (the best way of all to learn), and you've got to observe and emulate those who win. Still, I like to think that this book will be extremely helpful because of its emphasis on those essentials of winning that are so often overlooked. If you are an experienced, active, and good sailor, I'm hopeful that this book will allow you to reach new plateaus of achievement. If you are already a world-class sailor, you just might increase your awareness of why you win and thereby become even better. In short, this is a book designed to help those at any level.

Let's take a look at these keys to racing success that make a complicated sport relatively simple and that could elevate you to the winner's circle.

2

PREPARE

I can sense your disappointment. You've gotten through the first chapter and were looking forward to a few hot new tips on how to become an instant winner. Then the very next chapter is on the boring subject of preparation. "Everyone knows you've got to prepare a racing boat to win. I've been doing it for years," you're saying to yourself. "What's new in that?"

What is new is that unless you are a very rare breed, unless you're already a winner in the big time, you are not preparing well enough or hard enough, neither your boat nor yourself.

You probably feel that if you have a good boat with a smooth bottom and good sails you're in business. When I was growing up, that was sufficient. But no longer! Being a lazy type, I hate working on preparation. I always have, but now, in the twilight of my racing career, I know how much that has hurt me. One of the outstanding sailors I've enjoyed racing against is Bill Cox— the only sailor to win three U.S.Y.R.U. Championships, the Sears Cup (national junior championship), the Mallory Cup (national senior championship), and the Prince of Wales Bowl (national match-racing championship). Sometimes I manage to beat Bill, but more often he beats me. In retrospect I feel that, while he may be a better sailor once the race starts (I'm not quite willing to admit that), I know he is better at getting ready. When we both had Lightnings, Bill spent hours with his sailmaker checking one suit of sails against another, then recutting and testing again. It couldn't have hurt. In contrast, I tuned my boat while sailing out to the line for the start of the first race of the season and didn't have enough time to finish the job. When we got hooked up against each other on the last leg of the race, guess who had better boat speed.

One year I got even. In 1964 Bill and I were racing against each other for the defender's role in the America's Cup. I was sailing *Constellation,* and he was skipper of *American Eagle.* In an America's Cup campaign it's traditional that you sail every day for months on end. Far more time is spent readying the boat and crew than racing her. There is no chance to be lazy, and even if you wanted to be, neither the crew nor custom would allow it. Hence, *Constellation* was ready. Day after day we had the sailmaker check our sails, and by the time they had been recut a dozen times they had reached perfection. Every piece of gear was put and maintained in perfect working order. The crew was kept fit by daily running and exercise. Hours of drill under sail were followed by an early curfew each night. The bottom was massaged almost every day though we berthed overnight in a boat bath to make growth of organisms on the surface impossible. Bill, of course, was doing the same thing, but at least he didn't have an edge in preparation. We did have a slight edge in boat speed—not much, but just enough. I'm sure we wouldn't have beaten *American Eagle* if we hadn't prepared *Constellation,* her sails, and her crew to near perfection.

I say near perfection because a few years later an even better way was thought of to prepare the Twelves for battle. They were dry-sailed. Hauled out after every race, the boats had their bottoms smoothed to absolute perfection. When I was racing the aluminum-hulled *Courageous* against the wooden-hulled *Intrepid* in 1974, I figured that we would gain an edge as the summer wore on and *Intrepid* soaked up a bit of weight. I hadn't counted on the fact that not only would *Intrepid* be dry-sailed, but also that every night there would be heat lamps in her to dry her out, keeping her as light as when she was first launched. At the end of the summer, she had not settled even a sixteenth of an inch on her lines. She had to be beaten on the race course, not off it, because she was in a perfect state of readiness.

Let's talk for a moment about the importance of a smooth bottom, something we all know. On *Courageous* we had what I thought was a perfect bottom. It felt smoother than my Lightning's bottom ever had, and it looked perfect too, without a blemish. I was surprised, therefore, when Olin Stephens insisted that we spend a whole day wet-sanding it with the finest paper before the final trials. We had been doing just that all summer long, but Olin felt it could be improved. Apparently, even after hours of sanding, there are hollows and imperfections that only a microscope could detect. Moreover, Olin assured me that it is impossible to overemphasize the importance of a supersmooth bottom in making a boat go faster. A dozen of us spent an entire

GREG DORLAND

The importance of a smooth bottom cannot be overemphasized. This one is bottle-smooth, but the skipper is smart to be checking the bottom of the keel, which is often rough since it bears the boat's weight when sitting on a trailer. It might also have been scarred by going aground. Make it all smooth—supersmooth.

day working on a bottom that seemed perfect when we started. I'll take Olin's word for the fact that it made us faster, but I suspect it did something else for us: it prepared us mentally. When we raced the next day, there was one thing we didn't have to worry about. We knew we had a bottom as smooth as mortal man could make it, and we felt invincible. That state of euphoria lasted all through the next five races, four of which we managed to win.

Paul Elvström of Denmark has set a record in small-boat racing that may never be equaled—four Olympic gold medals and twelve world championships. He is, of course, a consummate sailor, but he also has a formula for success, which he calls P^6. It translates as follows: "Proper Prior Preparation Prevents Poor Performance." Paul means more than preparing the boat, which he does as painstakingly as anyone I know. He prepares himself too. Before winning his first Olympic medal in Finns, he had rigged a contraption to his bathtub to practice hiking. All winter long he spent untold hours each day hiking out. When the racing started he was so fit he could continue hiking longer than anyone else. He could better concentrate on boat speed and tactics since he wasn't hurting the way the others were.

All top-flight sailors now exercise by running and bicycling, and with special drills to simulate hiking. If you don't (I don't), you are at a disadvantage.

Elvström feels you've got to be mentally ready too. He feels anyone not at peace with himself, say from an unhappy marriage or any other disturbance, has two strikes against him. It takes total concentration and dedication to sail really well. If you're bothered by other matters, you cannot perform at your best. That's why it's so important to have fun while sailing—not frivolous fun, but a joyous feeling about what you are doing. It helps concentration, helps you to think straight, and keeps you loose in your movements.

As good as Buddy Melges is, I doubt that he would have stepped into the Star Class and won back-to-back world championships had he not devised ways to prepare his boat better. Stars had been sailing for over sixty years, and one might have expected all of the secrets to have been learned. Still, Buddy developed unique methods of backstay handling and other efficient ways to improve handling and control of the rig and gear. You don't have to be an engineer to do this, but you must, after the likes of Melges have pointed the way, emulate them so that your boat is equally prepared and perfected.

Dennis Conner owns two Stars, both good. One might be a shade better in heavy air, the other better in light, but the real virtue of owning two boats is to have a friendly trial horse. He gets another good sailor to steer one of the boats. By swapping sails and keeping an accurate log of their performance, he knows for sure which sails are best in various wind strengths. You don't have to own two boats to do this; you can brush with a friend who has a fine boat and it will help both of you to determine optimum-performance settings.

Prior to winning his last world championship in the Star Class in 1977, Dennis prepared in a unique way. The series was to be held at Kiel, an area of predominantly heavy air. Dennis went on a crash eating program and gained forty pounds. It turned out that it didn't blow very hard after all, but if it had, Dennis would have been ready. He had also figured out that, even in moderate air, Stars gained more from a heavy crew than they might lose in light air. Quite frankly, I'm not going to change my diet to suit the wind conditions. But this shows what we mortals are up against, and it proves, I hope, how important it is to be prepared in every sense. Dennis looked like hell after his eating program, but he won.

The consequences of improper preparation are often painful. Next time your spinnaker halyard jams in the sheave, ask yourself whether, if you had inspected it beforehand, you wouldn't have found it to have opened up a bit. When your jib sheet breaks, you know as well as I do that, unless it was undersized to start with, it had frayed through usage and you were unprepared by not having replaced it. When your sails split at the seams, blame only yourself for not having had them resewn *before* they split. If the first time you race your new boat in a heavy breeze all sorts of things break or you generally muck it up, don't blame it on the fact that you hadn't a chance to test her before the season started. The winners find the time.

I've raced with Bob Derecktor on a number of his boats, some of them so new that they had never been raced before their maiden starts in the S.O.R.C. in February. Still, I cannot ever recollect anything breaking down. One reason for this is that Bob is a superlative builder. Another is that all his new boats are properly shaken down *before* they race, no matter how difficult it

These two experienced sailors know the importance of going aloft to tape spreader ends to prevent chafe and to check rigging. Breakdowns happen only to those who don't prepare.

PETER BARLOW

might be to find the opportunity. For example, a boat is completed and launched up north in November. Bob takes her out and brushes with her predecessors to remove the bugs and to detect any shortcomings. One December day it was blowing forty-five knots, snowing hard with the thermometer reading twenty-five degrees Fahrenheit. Bob realized it was a great day to wring her out. He went out with a crew shanghaied from his yard. She had a coal-burning stove in the cabin, where the crew thawed out between sail changes. Thus was mutiny averted. Some things did go wrong, but this severe testing prevented mishaps when she raced two months later. As a further shake-down, he always sails his boats south in the dead of winter. This is not a smart thing to do unless you have an especially stout boat and experienced crew, but it is a very smart thing for Bob to do to insure that his boat and crew are fully prepared for the worst the Southern Circuit races might dish up. His new boats are better prepared than many year-old models, whose owners avoid pretesting them in severe weather. It is possible to complete a number of races without once experiencing tough conditions. Bob's theory is to seek out the tough weather before racing so that deficiencies and snafus will surface in time to correct them beforehand, rather than lose points through break-downs in an actual race.

Dennis Conner, in his 1978 book *No Excuse to Lose,* when writing about Lowell North, who he then considered the world's best all-around sailor, said:

> Like myself, he probably doesn't think of himself as endowed with a great deal of natural sailing ability, but he and I both know that natural ability isn't every-thing. Practice, not natural ability, teaches you how to round a mark properly and how to trim a sail. Lowell is a fanatic about boat preparation and equipment.

This emphasis on preparation and practice (see Chapter 3) has elevated Lowell above the rank-and-file good sailors into a select group at the very top. It is also revealing that Conner doesn't believe himself to be endowed with great natural ability either. Instead, he credits hard work, attention to detail, and unending practice for elevating him into the company of the world's best.

I attribute Carleton Mitchell's success with *Finisterre* to the superb way she was prepared. *Finisterre* won three consecutive Bermuda Races and many concluded that she must have been a superior boat. I don't agree. She was a lovely boat, she did fit the rule nicely, but the same could be said of many of her competi-tors. *Finisterre* won because Mitch had her outfitted superbly and lined up a most experienced and able crew. This paid off particularly in her third victory in 1960. With just one hundred miles to go, *Finisterre* was not close to winning. Then on the last night out a full gale hit the fleet, with gusts up to sixty knots. This was the chance *Finisterre* was waiting for. Her great crew kept her driving throughout the night and none of her gear failed. Meanwhile a great many other boats hove to. I was racing on Fred Adam's *Katama* and before the storm hit we had a winning margin on *Finisterre*. We also had a great crew, but when *Katama* started leaking so much that we had trouble keeping up with it, despite bailing with a pump and two buckets, Fred decided quite wisely that we better heave to in order to guard against *Katama*'s breaking up. When we did, little water came in, and hence after a couple of hours we got under way again. Despite the time we lost, we still won our class; but we had lost our chance to beat *Finisterre*. We found out later that the water was coming through a hole just below the transom where the backstay chainplate was attached. It wasn't a new hole and it didn't impair *Katama*'s strength. Only when being driven hard in extreme conditions did it get sufficiently underwater to cause a leak. Had we prepared properly, we would have sought out extreme conditions to test *Katama* or we would have made a thorough hull inspection. Having done neither, we lost all chance of beating *Finisterre*.

By now you might well be a bit discouraged by the extremes that top sailors go to in preparing for a race. Most sailors, even the good ones, don't go this far. I sure don't, and I've done pretty well. Even some of the outstanding sailors are not willing, or don't have the time, to make such a commitment; but there

Even in a simple production boat like a Sunfish preparation pays off. Note extras such as compass, course and wind plotter, grease pencil and holder, and sight lines for tacking and mast-abeam positioning. Note also the unique daggerboard retainer, mainsheet lead, custom hiking shorts, and dual stopwatches. The galaxy of chevrons proves that preparation paid off. This Sunfish belongs to North American champion Carl Knight.

are two messages I would like to leave with you. First, if you aspire to winning in world-class competition, you *must* make such an all-out effort in preparing. If you don't, someone just as good as you, but no better, will beat you. Second, if you are unable or unwilling to take the time for such total commitment, and you do your racing on a more local level, one sure way to move up in the standings is to prepare a lot better than you have been. If not carried to extremes, preparation can be enjoyable and will lead to the greater pleasure that will surely ensue from doing better on the race course. It's discouraging to lose because of inferior equipment or inadequate preparation. There is no surer way to move up the ladder than to prepare better than that guy who is no smarter and no more experienced than you, but who heretofore was better prepared. If you're not willing to go even that far, seek out an easy class where no one takes the racing seriously, resign yourself to trailing the pack, or give up racing altogether.

But should you aspire to success in the big-time classes and events, bear in mind that you don't have a chance of winning with any regularity unless you observe the first key by being prepared, *really* prepared. It's the foundation without which you will never rise to the top.

3

PRACTICE

You have just digested the somewhat distasteful news that to improve your sailing you've got to spend more time and effort in preparation than suits your fancy. You know from the heading of this chapter that the next key to success is practice. Once again you feel it's something you already know, and once again I've got to tell you that you simply don't give adequate credit to the importance of practicing, whatever your level of competence. But take heart. This will be a short chapter, because I think I can prove the point rather quickly. Take heart also from the fact that practicing can be fun.

Practice is really the final form of preparation prior to racing, and it could have been covered in the previous chapter. I have chosen not to do so because it's a different type of preparation worth scrutiny on its own.

It's obvious to beginners that they have to practice the basic evolutions of tacking, jibing, and just plain sailing. It's obvious, too, that they will benefit from more hours sailing through seas, from learning how to keep a boat on her feet in a hard wind, and from keeping her moving in light air without driving off too much. Unless you've got an experienced crew, it should be apparent that lots of practice in spinnaker work and headsail changes will be helpful.

Is there any set pattern for practicing? Not really. It's important, of course, to go through all the evolutions you will encounter in a race. If you get someone else to take his boat out, you can even practice starts against each other by setting up a line between two moored boats and coordinating your watches. You should concentrate on your weakest areas. If you do poorly in heavy air, then it is doubly important to go out on windy days. Again it will be more helpful if you have a trial horse to sail against to gauge your progress, but you will benefit even without one. Jibing in a real gale can be precarious, but if it's not blowing too hard for racing, it is extremely helpful to go through enough jibes so that you will feel comfortable.

I once overdid this. It was the year my wife, Charlotte, and I were married and we were frostbiting in Interclub dinghies at Larchmont. It was blowing great guns but not too hard to race. We had never jibed our dinghy in such wind and I told Charlotte we had to practice jibes. We got through the first one, but on the second one we capsized. Imagine my chagrin to discover that in such wind the committee always signaled a no-jibe course! After being fished out of icy water we bailed out our dinghy, rushed to the clubhouse to change into dry clothing, and competed in all but the first race of the day. We nearly capsized in one of the races, which would have given us a frostbite record of capsizing twice in one day. With subsequent practice, however, we got pretty good at jibing in a hard blow.

By practicing your weaknesses often enough you can turn them into strengths. And just by putting hours of sailing under your belt you will become so attuned to your boat that when you get into a race your boat speed will take care of itself and you will be able to think more about the tactics of winning. Practice is vital at all levels of ability, a fact that becomes apparent by noting how important the very best sailors rate it.

A few months before the 1976 Olympics, I visited Peter Barrett, who had been a member of previous Olympic teams, and who was planning that year to enter the Olympic trials in the Tempest Class. Peter was a top contender, but in the previous autumn had hurt his leg. When I visited him, the leg was completely healed. It was early March, and the final trials were nearly three months off. I asked Peter how he rated his chances and was surprised to find him rather pessimistic. When I asked him why, he said he didn't feel he had sufficient time to practice. I assumed he had business commitments that would

Practice needed! A classic snafu that teamwork could have prevented. Note that the main has been dropped by accident in the effort to lower the spinnaker and clear the wrap.

interfere, but this was not the case. In fact, he and his crew were planning to sail together a few hours *every* day after work for the next two and a half months. "But I'm afraid that won't give us time to get really sharp," Peter said. Mind you, this was a world-class sailor speaking.

In 1979, a year before the America's Cup campaign, Dennis Conner sailed Twelves over five hundred hours (the equivalent of more than sixty eight-hour days). He practiced over fifteen hundred hours in the Cup year itself. Dennis is one of the best in the business with a crew composed of extremely experienced sailors. John Bertrand, the outstanding United States Finn sailor, has spent the last two years doing little other than sailing Finns all around the world. It's well known that once the ice left the harbor in Denmark, Paul Elvström used to go sailing regularly almost every day.

This lengthy practice by the best sailors should convince us all how vital it is. Once you learn to sail a boat well and have developed a feel for making her go, it's something that never leaves you. Still, the more you sail, the more you get attuned to your boat. The two of you become almost one. It becomes instinctive to keep her in the groove. You learn how to play the waves just a shade better, how to tack and jibe most efficiently. You also develop an ability to detect wind shifts and to gauge the velocity of approaching puffs. If you are already good, you won't be much better after this extensive practice, but *you will be better*. Even a slight edge can make all the difference in keen competition. In boats with large crews, practice is the only way to develop teamwork. It's a joy to race with a Twelve Meter crew at the end of a summer's campaign. The most impossible evolutions become routine.

Most of us simply aren't going to practice to any such degree. But if those who are already expert sailors consider practice so important, doesn't it follow that it should be of even greater help to the average good sailor and to beginners? To realize *most* of the improvement it's not necessary to practice for days or weeks on end. Be honest with yourself. If you are at all typical, you might practice with your crew (excluding racing) just a few days all summer. Tripling the amount of time will pay tremendous dividends without making you a slave to the sport.

In fact, at the risk of scuttling my arguments about how important practice is, let me point out that many great sailors simply don't find time to do a great deal of it, but they, like

Without practice there's no way this spinnaker could be drawing before leaving the mark, no way four men could be so well positioned to drop the jib with a rush while a fifth mans the halyard. Note the level pole. A set like this will gain two boat lengths or more over a sloppy one.

anyone else, will benefit by an increase in practice. Jim Crane, who won the Lightning North Americans in 1979, credited much of his success to the fact that for the first time in several years he had been able to practice with his crew for seven days.

The point is that most sailors practice very little. Yet, when certain dedicated experts consider it so vital, shouldn't you and I at least do it more than we do at present? There are few easier ways to show marked improvement. The improvement will encounter diminishing returns as the amount of practice passes a certain point, but it's always ascending and so is very worthwhile if you really care about doing better on the race course.

4

THINK LOW ON A REACH

*A*t last we've come to the simple sort of key move you've been hoping for—one that, if you have the guts and judgment to employ it properly, is almost guaranteed to improve your race record on any level of competition. The overwhelming majority of sailors, even good ones, tend to sail too high on reaching legs and as a consequence lose a great deal toward the end of the leg. If upon reaching the windward mark and starting the reach you use every opportunity to sail lower than the fleet, you will almost always gain.

This simple tactic works because of human nature. The lead boat usually sails a bit high to keep close pursuers from driving over her. The pursuers also tend to sail high partly in hopes of blanketing and then passing the leader, and partly to protect themselves from being blanketed and passed by those behind. Unless it is blowing hard and the reach is a very tight one, a boat will go faster by sailing high of the course. Knowledge of this fact forces almost everyone up above the rhumb line.

It's not easy to go low. If you do, you will sail slower. You are apt to be blanketed, and in a tightly bunched fleet you are apt to lose several places in the first quarter mile of the leg. But by this time, if you've played your cards properly, you will be far enough to leeward of the pack to be affected no longer. Thereafter, you can sail your own race, driving off below the rhumb line in the puffs, going a bit above it in the lulls. In so doing you will not only be sailing the shortest distance, but you will also be sailing it at top speed. The pack to windward of you won't have this freedom. They will be afraid to drive off in the puffs, for fear of being blanketed. Hence, the first two-thirds of the leg will be spent sailing even higher, getting farther and farther high of the course, sailing a pronounced curve between the two marks.

Eventually the moment of truth will come. Everyone has to bear off for the mark, but unless the wind has increased a great deal, they all will go much slower as they fight their way down. Moreover, they can no longer protect against blanketing. If they do, they will get even higher and lose more still when the time comes that they must bear off to round the mark.

If you're well to leeward of this unfortunate pack, it's a joyous sight to see them slowing down and blanketing each other while you recoup far more than what you lost initially by sailing low early in the leg. If the wind lightens late in the leg, the leeward boat will gain even more. But even if the wind remains steady, you are absolutely sure to gain. You will have sailed a shorter distance, and you will have been able to sail your own fastest course. See figures 1a, b, and c.

I called this chapter "Think Low on a Reach" rather than "Sail Low on a Reach" because there are times when it will kill you to sail low initially. If you have good reason to believe that the wind will increase as the leg progresses, or if you can see a line of stronger wind up to weather, you should sail high early in the leg. If after you've gone low early in the leg you detect better wind up high, then you should take your medicine and cut your losses by getting back up with the pack. If you don't detect better wind up to weather and expect neither an increase nor decrease in wind velocity throughout the leg, all your thoughts should be focused on getting low early, although you will lose ground initially. I can guarantee that you will sail a shorter course than the others. You will have gained ground by the time the leg is over—sometimes not a big gain, but almost always a significant one. Should the wind lighten in the latter part of the leg, your gain will be tremendous.

Maybe you are still skeptical and suspicious that this tack is risky and often unproductive. Maybe you feel it will work only against a fleet of poor or inexperienced sailors. To prove my

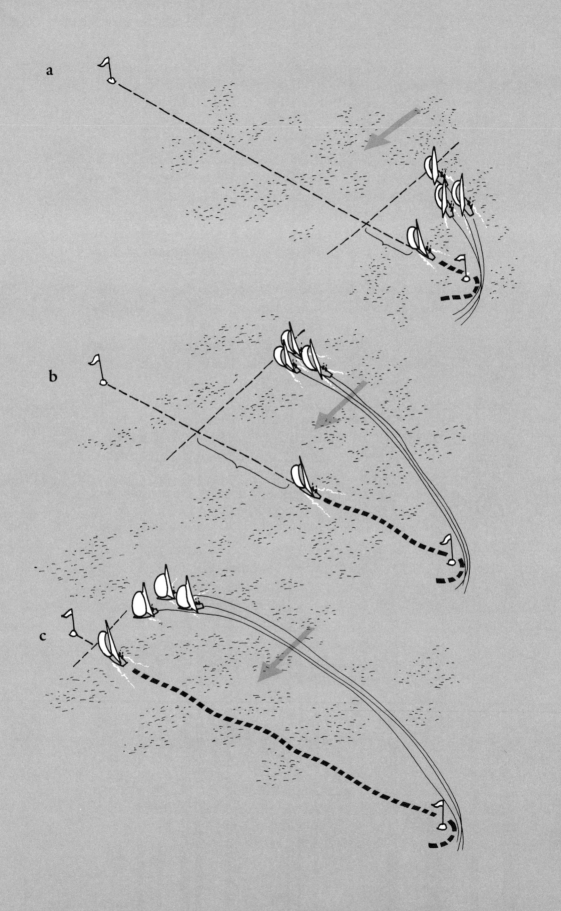

a

b

c

point, let me illustrate how it has worked for me, how it has failed, and how I've seen it work for others at the highest level of competition.

I first learned this key tactic from my dad, both by watching him win with it when I crewed for him and also by having had it drummed into my mind by listening to him explain why and how it worked. The first time I employed it with phenomenal success was when I was fifteen years old and racing Triangle Class sloops off Gloucester, Massachusetts, in the Sears Cup finals. I had never sailed Triangles before, was unfamiliar with the waters, and had great trouble sailing the boat upwind against the prevailing slop and light-to-moderate weather. After four races I was last in the fleet of eight—not a distant last—but still I stood eighth, not exactly the place to be with just four races to go. I had been rounding the weather mark either last or close to it, and despite gaining a place or two downwind, my goose seemed cooked. I was beginning to get the hang of getting Triangles upwind, and in the last four races was rounding the weather mark between third and fifth—not good but at least within striking distance. I came very close to winning the fifth race, and did win the last three. I did it in each case by sailing low on the reaches and blasting through at the end. I wish I were able to report that I thereby won the Sears Cup, but I had put myself in too big a hole in the first four races and was still two points out of first when the series ended. Still, I got real joy from the reaction of the other juniors who couldn't quite fathom how that young squirt who was never really up there at the windward mark, "where races are supposed to be won and lost," had come so very close to winning.

FIGURE 1

a

The first three boats are sailing high of the course to keep their wind clear. The fourth boat, being blanketed and sailing a slower angle to the wind, drops back.

b

The reach is now half over and the boat on the rhumb line has dropped even farther back. But now she has her wind clear and has freedom to wiggle, going up in the light spots, down in the puffs.

c

In the latter part of the reach the boats that sailed high pay the price. They go very slowly as they square off to get down to the mark. The boat that has hewed to the rhumb line and sailed a shorter course now gets her reward as she charges through their lee on a fast point of sail.

*These four Solings are all holding high starting the reach, intent on keep-
ing a clear wind. A boat immediately behind them would be smart to bear
off instead of following.*

Most of these Solings have held high and are slowing down as they start to bear off for the mark. Note the boat to leeward, which is charging through many of them on a fast point of sail.

"Okay, it will work with kids," I can hear you saying, "but will it work in top-level competition?" You bet it will. If you will accept the fact that Olympic fleets aren't too shabby, I can prove it. I was a member of the International Jury for the 1976 Olympics at Kingston. After watching the Solings for a while, we shifted to the 470 course. The 470s had rounded the weather mark and were halfway down the reaching leg. We situated ourselves at the jibe mark and could sight right along the reaching leg. "Wonder who that is so far to leeward?" another judge asked me. "I don't know," I said, "but I do know he is the only one sailing a straight leg. Bet he gains a heap." The leg was half over, and the boat in question was at least two hundred yards to leeward of everyone else. But from our vantage point we could see that he was directly on the rhumb line. Everyone else had been sucked up high, either attacking or protecting themselves from attack. As they neared the jibe mark, the lone boat to leeward of the fleet came charging through to round in third place. In the Olympics careful records of boat placement are taken at each mark. By checking them I found that our friend had rounded the weather mark in twelfth place, picking up nine places on the reach! He eventually faded to sixth because he didn't have top boat speed. But he knew this key to racing success, and he played it for all it was worth against the world's best sailors.

It also works in distance racing. The two-hundred-mile Block Island Race, from Larchmont, New York, and around Block Island and back, starts in the late afternoon. In those waters and at that time of day the prevailing wind is a southwesterly, usually a rather fresh one. This gives a reach down the Long Island Sound with the rhumb-line course taking you straight down the middle. Does the fleet sail down the middle? Not on your life! The vast majority hold high, hugging the Long Island shore, keeping their wind clear and going like gangbusters. A few brave souls do hew to the rhumb line. I almost always do, and for the first three hours it is tough to take. Boats of the same rating as mine are invariably up ahead, a few miles to windward, but a mile or more ahead of us. Then the sun sets, and soon after dark the wind starts to abate. You can almost count on it. By this time the Long Island shore keeps boats to weather from sailing higher to freshen their wind. Instead, they have to bear off in winds lighter than those they used to get up there. You know what happens as well as I do. They die coming down and the few boats in the middle, whether they hew to the rhumb-line course or whether they now sail high of it to bring the apparent wind still closer in the lighter air, increase speed dramatically. See figure 2.

In one Block Island Race, which we eventually won in my thirty-footer *Memory,* we were the smallest and lowest-rated boat among the more than one hundred entries. Just before it got dark we were so far behind the next to last boat that we could no longer recognize her. But that night, as the boats ahead began dying when forced to bear off, we had the time of our life watching the lights of bigger, faster boats on our weather bow drop back and finally drop onto our quarter. By next morning we were ahead of thirty-seven of them, all of which gave us time.

Does this always work? No, not always. I've sailed in twenty-eight of these races with a southwesterly wind at the start, and have always sailed the rhumb line early under such conditions. Twenty-six times we have made huge gains after dark. The other two times we ran flat in the middle while the fleet held a shore breeze and was out of sight ahead the next morning. I'll take those odds of thirteen to one any day. If I had been smarter and a bit less stubborn in the two instances in which it did backfire so miserably, maybe I could have salvaged respectability by sharpening up dramatically when I first saw the lights to windward drawing still farther ahead instead of dropping back as expected.

Another time my strategy backfired was in the last race of the 1979 Block Island Week. I was racing my J-30, and the first leg was a reach to the Rhode Island shore. Everyone held high. I did a bit, too, but was still way below the rest. For a while it seemed to be okay, but then I saw a stronger wind line up to windward. I was slow in reacting, figuring it would come down to us in due time. It never did. By not taking my medicine and reaching up to be close behind at the first mark, I was instead a dirty last. I got some satisfaction by staying low on the next reach, thereby getting back into the middle of the fleet. Still, I kicked myself for sticking to an accepted doctrine when the prevailing conditions were shouting to me that this time it simply was not going to work.

One more example of a sensational success employing this tactic occurred when I was sailing my Soling in the Atlantic Coast Championship off Annapolis. I had done a lousy job of calling the fickle, shifting winds. When we rounded the last

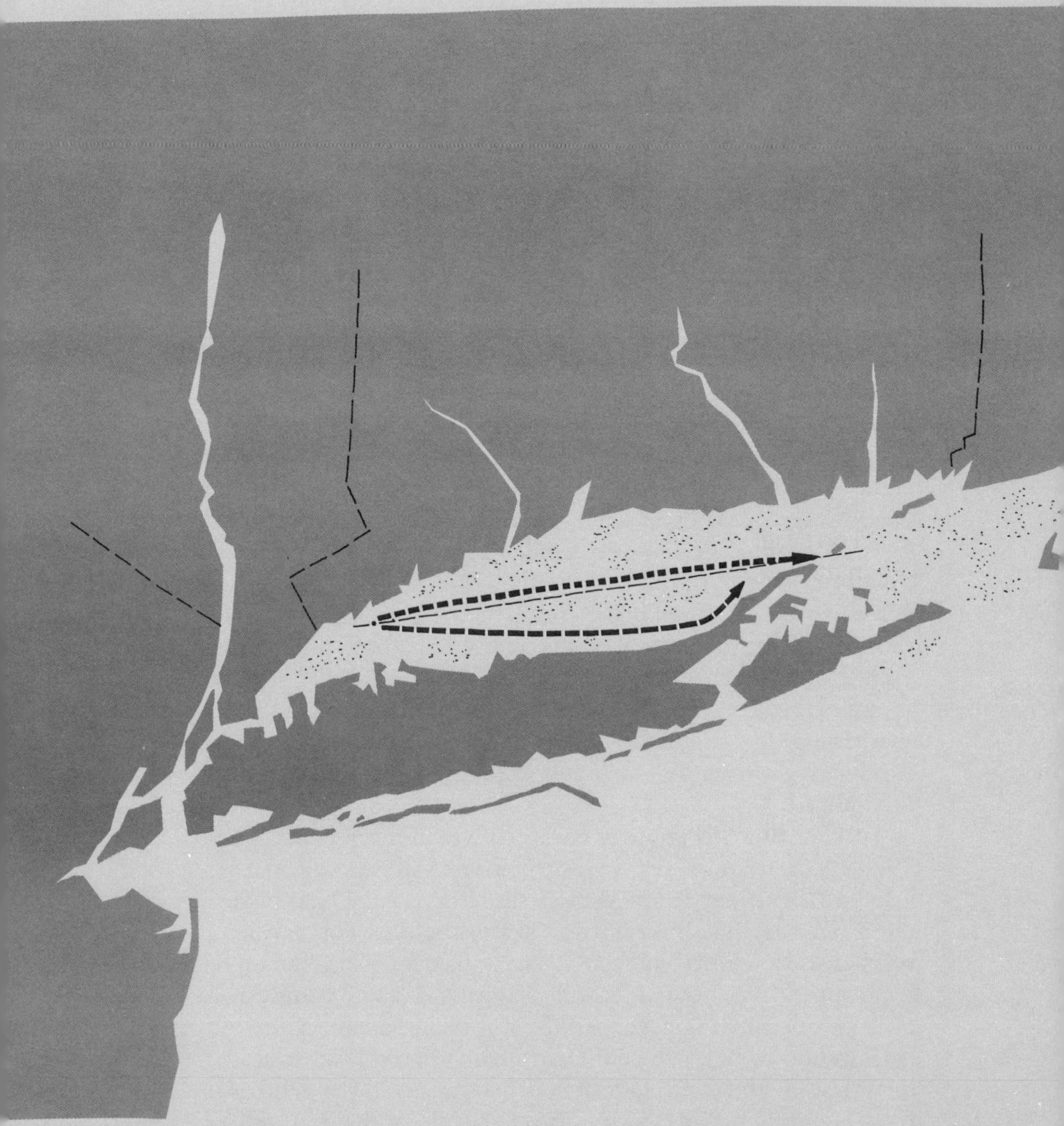

FIGURE 2

The dark dotted line parallel to the rhumb line shows the course I prefer with the sou'wester at the start of the Block Island Race. The dark dotted line close to the Long Island shore shows the course a larger portion of the fleet takes. The fleet will gain early, but as the wind abates after dark (as it usually does) the land forces them to bear off at the very time we start heading up. Everyone knows you should bear off in the puffs and up in the light stuff, but unless you think low on this long reach you will do just the opposite.

mark, it was a tight reach to the finish. We were in an unenviable eighteenth place at the turn, and things looked hopeless, particularly since the leader was a full half-mile ahead with but a two-and-a-half-mile reach to go. As we approached the last mark, we noted that the fleet ahead of us heading for home was sailing a bit high of the course to get a bit of money in the bank in case of a header. We noted also that the current was setting to windward, and that the wind was beginning to lighten. Partly because of our hopeless position, and partly because there were hard reasons why it just might work, when we rounded we didn't hold high. Instead we set a spinnaker, and drove off ten degrees below the course for home. It couldn't have worked better. The wind did continue to die. The current thereby became more of a factor, and crabbed us back up close to the rhumb line. Then came the frosting on the cake when the wind began to free us. By now all the boats up ahead and to weather had also set spinnakers. However, we had a faster sailing angle, and they were bucking current to get down. Hence, they had to sail much broader than they would have liked to maintain boat speed. See figures 3a, b, and c.

Did we win? No, not quite. But we were overlapped with the winner. The leader at the last mark, the leader over us by half a mile, wound up five places behind us. A bit of a fluke? Of course, but if the wind hadn't faired, we still would have gained, although not as many places.

More important than this extreme example is the certainty that in the vast majority of cases if you will think hard about getting below the fleet on a reach, and find no hard reasons against doing so under the conditions at hand, you will gain—sometimes dramatically, sometimes just a little, but gain you will.

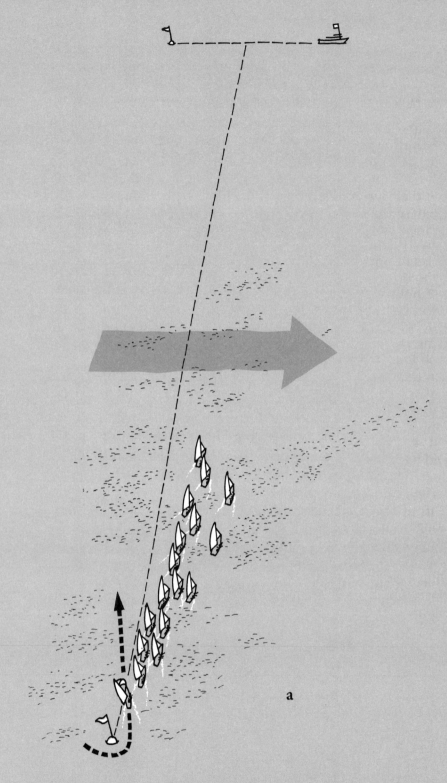

a

FIGURE 3

We were in this "hopeless" position (dark dotted line) starting a tight reach for home in the Soling Atlantic Coast Championship. We set a chute and drove off to leeward.

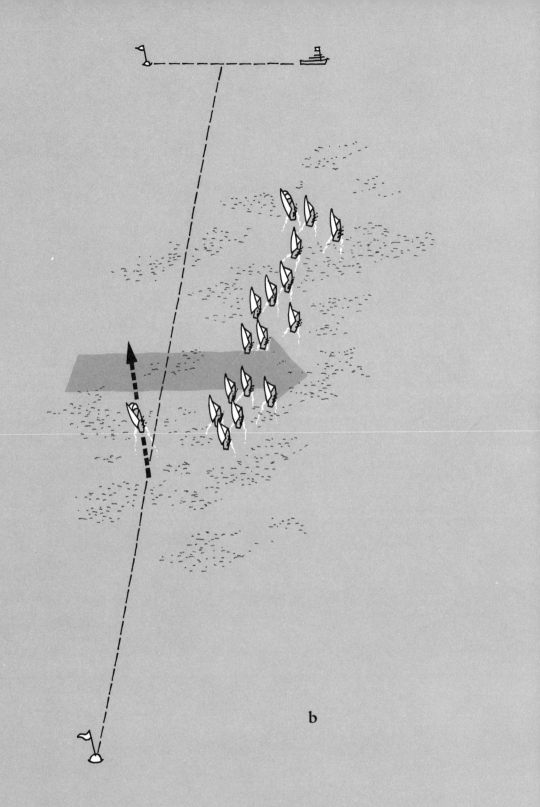

b

Halfway down the leg, things began to look brighter. Current was crabbing us almost up to the finish line and the wind was lightening all over.

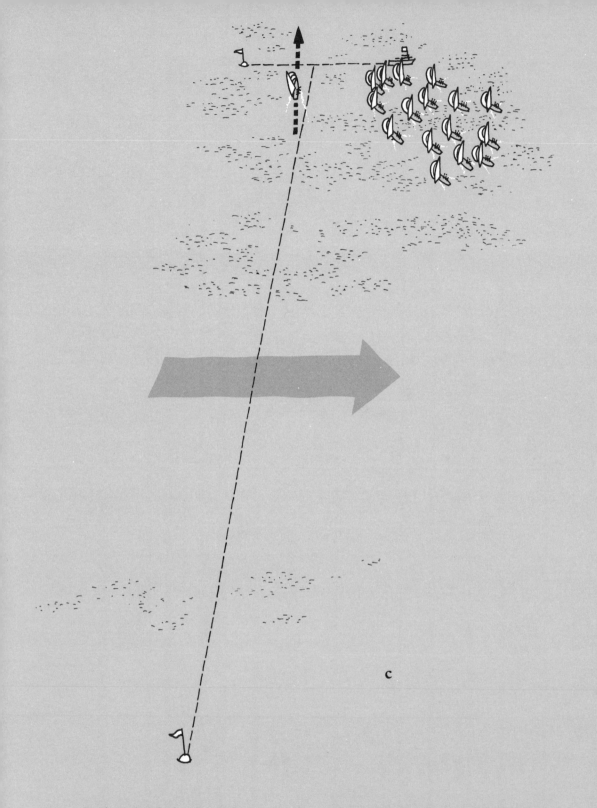

c

By the end of the leg the wind was very light and had faired. The fleet had trouble bucking the current to get down to the finish, while we had a fast angle. I've never seen "thinking low" work better. We nearly won.

5

LOSE A LITTLE TO SAVE A LOT

Salty Goose was broad-reaching for Fastnet Rock, which was some twenty miles ahead. We hadn't had a sight for over twelve hours. When thick fog rolled in, cutting visibility to little more than a hundred yards, I became a bit apprehensive. There is no radio beacon on the Fastnet, but there is one approximately nine miles past it, which we were homing in on. It shouldn't, therefore, have been too great a problem to find the rock, but still I was worried that we might sail past without seeing it. To port of the rock was deep water, too deep to get soundings. But just a few hundred yards to starboard of the direct course, the hundred-fathom curve arched out several miles toward us, shoaling gradually as one neared the Fastnet.

I told Bob Derecktor that I was concerned about trying to head directly for it. If we were just a bit to port of the course, we would get no soundings and might miss it altogether. I suggested we hold purposely high of course until we got on soundings, and then use subsequent soundings, coupled with RDF bearings, to pinpoint our position. We could then bear off for the Fastnet and find it for sure, even in this miserable visibility.

Bob bought the idea immediately, but our navigator was adamant. "That would make us lose up to two minutes because of the extra distance sailed," he said. "No need to do that. I'm sure we can find it just through the RDF bearing. Besides, the one-hundred-fathom curve does intersect our direct course close to the rock, so we will know when we are almost there." He was so positive and had such a reputation as an experienced navigator that Bob and I both gave in, though I don't think either of us was especially happy.

Up to weather, we could hear voices and the occasional grind of winches on *Charisma*. We knew that both of us were doing well, and if we could just shake *Charisma*, even though the Fastnet Race was just half over, we had illusions already of maybe, just maybe, taking home all the marbles.

Our ETA was 11:30 and we should have hit the hundred-fathom curve ten minutes sooner. When 11:30 came and still no soundings, Bob and I became really worried. The chart showed that if we were just a bit to port of course we would never get soundings until well past. We were worried also because RDF bearings had shown we were being set to port. True, we had corrected, but I later found that the navigator corrected only for the set we had experienced, not allowing for any future set we might encounter. The navigator remained calm on the exterior, avowing that we must be running behind our DR (dead reckoning), but throughout the race we had been exceeding our estimated speed and that which the log showed. By now we could no longer hear *Charisma* and were worried sick.

After a few minutes more of studying the chart and pondering the possibilities, Bob told the navigator we were heading up. We sharpened up a full thirty degrees, but it was a full twenty minutes before we got on soundings, and a few minutes later, at 11:55, we saw a rocky shore. It took us a few minutes more to sort out the pieces and to ascertain that this shore was running not in the direction it should be prior to reaching the Fastnet, but instead could be only the shore beyond it. The awful truth was that instead of being behind our DR we were ahead of it, and were already well past the Fastnet when we had sharpened up. See figure 4.

We were a grim crew as we reached back. We found the rock and then had to circle it to leave it on the correct side. By "saving one or two minutes," we had lost well over an hour, rounding at 12:45.

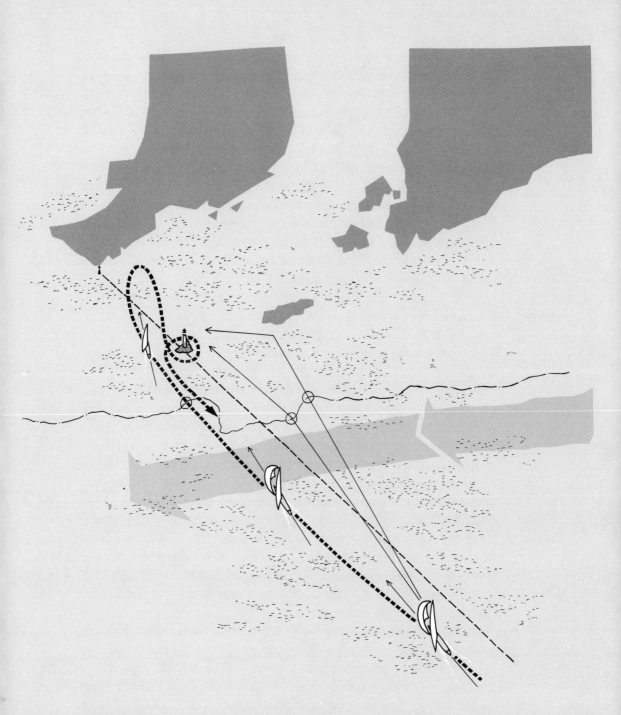

FIGURE 4

The dark dotted line represents Salty Goose's course when she missed the Fastnet. The course to windward of her would have intercepted the hundred-fathom curve (which Goose just missed) and would have told us how far we were from the light, thus making it easier to find it. The most windward course, pursued till land was sighted, would have taken a couple more minutes to sail, but would have made it a cinch to find the Fastnet. The course we sailed, in an attempt to lose no distance, made us lose over one hour.

We came home like gangbusters, wound up fourth in the fleet of 270 boats, and missed winning the most prestigious of all ocean races by twenty minutes. This remains the most bitter pill I've ever had to swallow in years of ocean racing, and is for me the quintessential example of the ocean racer's lament "We had it won, if only . . ." The "if only" in this case was entirely our own fault, with no shred of bad luck intervening. We deserved our fate. We had violated a key dictum of racing success: "Be willing to accept a slight loss whenever it can remove the possibility of incurring a big loss." It's just a question of evaluating the options and analyzing the pros and cons. Whenever one action, if unsuccessful, can result in disaster, latch onto another that will surely keep you in the ball game.

In this incident Bob and I blame each other as much as we do the navigator. It was Bob's job as skipper and my job as watch captain and tactician to overrule the navigator by choosing a course that would have kept us in the race instead of throwing it away with nearly three hundred miles to go.

Another time, a year or two earlier, in Bob's boat *Wild Goose*, we were willing to lose a little to save a lot, and save we did. We were reaching under spinnaker south of the Florida Keys in the Saint Petersburg–Fort Lauderdale Race. Next to us was our arch rival, *Salty Tiger*. It was midafternoon and to windward of us were the black clouds of an approaching front. It looked wicked, but sometimes there's little wind in such fronts. As it neared we were reluctant to lower our chute because this would let *Salty Tiger* jump us, at least momentarily. After a bit of discussion, we finally decided to douse, concluding that if the front held no great wind we could rehoist with only a few lengths lost. We had just set our heavy reaching jib and muzzled the chute when the front hit.

It not only blew a solid forty knots, but also shifted forward to make a close reach. *Wild Goose* took off like her namesake. By being willing to accept a slight loss, we had actually achieved a gain. We watched as *Salty Tiger*, which had elected to keep her spinnaker up, was first laid flat and then had to bear off at right angles to the course. By the time everything was under control, she had blown her spinnaker, buckled her pole, and sailed literally out of sight, last seen on our leeward quarter. We never saw her again in that race, and finished an hour ahead.

In a Miami–Nassau Race on *Salty Goose* a year after the Fastnet fiasco, we were conservative when, as it turned out, we

THE CORK EXAMINER

This is our forty-footer Witch *rounding the Fastnet (1971) under happier and easier conditions than when* Salty Goose *made her classic blunder.*

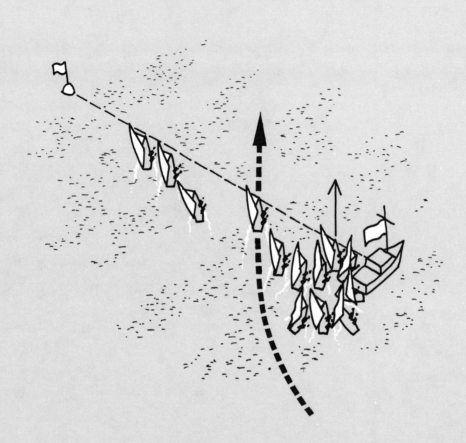

FIGURE 5

The dark dotted line shows a safe and effective start when the windward end is favored. One boat to windward has broken clear of the pack into a slight lead, but the conservative start has produced clear air and second place. That's much better than being the second boat at the favored end with bad air. By eschewing the best start you will save a lot on the boats that tried and failed to get the number-one start at the favored end.

need not have been. It was three in the morning, and we were running in moderate air from Stirrup direct for the finish. Behind us was a dark squall, lit only by great flashes of lightning. When the lightning illuminated the sea we couldn't see any great wind, just a wall of rain. Still, it looked so wicked we decided to lower spinnaker just before the squall reached us. We did and a minute or so later realized there was, if anything, less wind accompanied by a torrent of rain. A boat beside us had kept her chute up, and by the time we had rehoisted ours she had gained several lengths. It's my strong contention that even though we happened to be "wrong" in this instance we did the right thing. In the long run you're going to average out far better by being willing to accept a slight loss to avoid the possibility of a huge one caused by being reckless or greedy. In this particular race we lost little by playing it safe, and we eventually beat all the boats that had not lowered their spinnakers as the storm hit.

There's a difference between being chicken and being seamanlike. To win races, particularly today, you've got to press hard, carrying more sail downwind than you might feel really comfortable with. To do otherwise would be chicken, but beyond a certain point it becomes unseamanlike. It becomes stupid when you press on regardless, without first knowing that an approaching squall doesn't have a lot more wind than what you, your boat, or your sails can cope with. By so doing, you could lose a lot more than the race. Ocean racing needs no more fatalities than it has had in recent years.

The same key tactics of being willing to accept minor deficits to prevent big ones applies to closed-course racing. Few good sailors try always for the best start at the pin end of the line, even when it is favored. They realize that only one boat can get this best start, and that there is the danger of being over early, either by mistiming or by being forced over by boats just behind. A few superb starters will disagree with me, but the majority of fine sailors will take a start near the favored end, not at it. They think more of insuring that they can get clear air and of being well placed a minute after the start. Only one or two boats can be ahead at that stage, and they won't be far ahead. The race is young and you are well positioned to go to work on them. Trying for the best start and failing can put you way back in the pack—a tough position in a large, competitive fleet. See figure 5.

By the same token, it pays to tack short of laylines. Tacking right on the layline will save the distance otherwise lost by two tacks. However, if the winds head you, you will have to make two more tacks anyway. If it lifts, you will have lost even more through overstanding. If you're experienced, you already know these reasons for tacking short of the laylines, but too many experienced sailors still refuse to do it. The only explanation I know is that there is a reluctance to accept the minor loss of two extra tacks. However, this loss can be avoided only when you've timed your tack precisely and the wind remains steady thereafter. See figures 6a and b.

The wisdom of accepting two extra tacks applies also when you've got a comfortable lead and are starting the final weather leg. Say, for example, you have a 300-yard lead. After rounding go for 150 yards, then tack. See figure 7. After going around 150 yards, tack back. You will have lost a bit of ground by the two tacks, but you are now directly upwind of the second boat, directly between it and the finish. You've still got a huge lead, and if the wind shifts, no matter which way it shifts, you remain in a commanding position. We will talk a bit more about this particular situation in Chapter 8. For now please remember it as just another instance of being willing to lose a little to prevent the possibility of losing a lot.

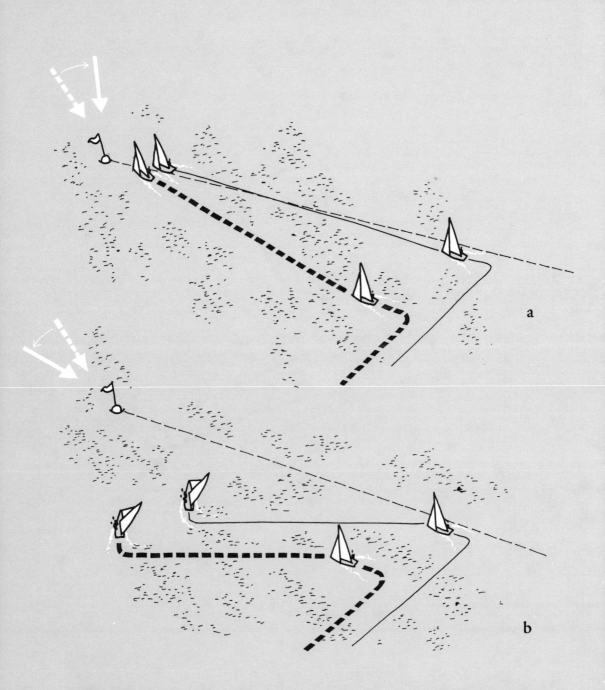

FIGURE 6

These two diagrams show the merit of tacking short of the lay line. If lifted (a) you will fetch and round first. If headed (b) you can then tack and cross and still round first. If the wind stays steady you will lose a little by taking two more tacks, but this is more than offset by the probability of rounding first if you are either lifted or headed—a good tradeoff.

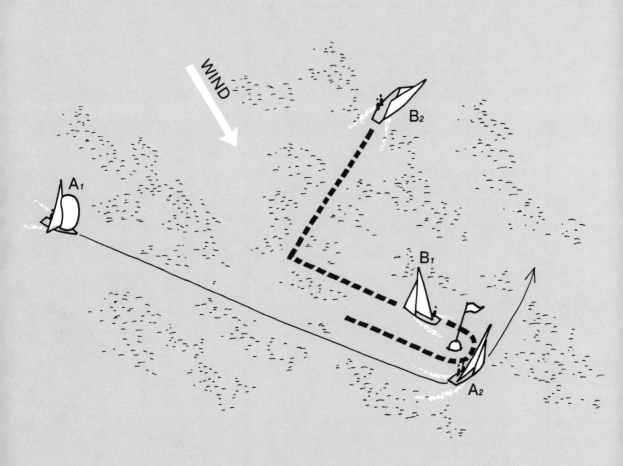

FIGURE 7

The little distance the lead boat loses by taking two tacks is more than offset by the fact that she is now between the second boat and the mark. By losing a little she is sure to retain her lead.

6

BE BOLD

ou have heard the saying "Faint heart never won fair lady." That's an area in which I am no expert, but I do know that the chickenhearted simply cannot win in sharp sailing competition. Being bold when you aren't truly competent can get you into horrendous trouble. But once your skills have matured, your confidence should build apace, and you should press on to win. If you don't, resign yourself to mediocre placings. Often the difference between winners and average sailors boils down to their different approach. The winner may be no more competent, except for the fact that he has more confidence, has a winning attitude, and attains his potential. I am not talking about being foolhardy. Trying things beyond your capabilities and beyond those of your boat and crew can lead to disaster. Even if it doesn't, it is apt to result in poorer finishes by exposing you to greater possibilities of fouling up. But, after analyzing the situation, if you think you can pull something off, it is well worth trying.

This is particularly obvious at starts. Often the difference between getting good starts and poor ones is purely one's mental attitude. Dennis Conner doesn't know anything more about getting good starts than a great many other experienced sailors. True, he has a good sense of timing and distance, but what makes him rank among the best starters in the world is his supreme confidence. He feels he is going to win the start, and he approaches that crucial part of the race with delight and a killer instinct. He doesn't always take the start, but by being bold he gets far more than his share. This applies to both fleet and match-race starts.

There's an easy rule of thumb to tell if you are being sufficiently bold at the start. If you enter thirty races and are never over early, you are not sufficiently bold. If you are a conservative starter, you will find it almost impossible to get over early; but by pressing more you are bound to get closer. Of course, I am not advocating premature starts, but one early start in thirty attempts is a small price to pay if the other twenty-nine are better than they would be otherwise.

Have you noticed as you cross the finish line that you expect to hear the whistle sooner than it actually comes? If there are ten people on board, ask them to indicate when they feel the bow has crossed the finish line. I can almost guarantee that nine of the ten (usually all ten) will call it prematurely. There's something that makes you sense you are on the line long before you are. A good way to check this is to face backward, looking at the starting line from the course side. When you sense you are near it, it will then appear that you are well on the starting side. Turn around and look at the line in the direction of the course. It will now appear that you are right on the line. Comparing the two sensations will give you assurance that you are not early. By practicing this exercise you will be better able to tell when you really are on the line. Then use that knowledge to press for better starts.

This knowledge is particularly useful if starting in the middle of a long starting line. You can be quite certain that there will be a big midline sag, simply because it is so difficult to tell when you are right on the line. In consequence, boats in the middle will almost surely be well short of the line. You can usually be at least a boat length ahead of the boats around you and still not be early. It takes guts to do this, and you will feel very naked out ahead of the pack, but you should be able to do it without being over early.

Proof of the importance of a bold and confident attitude at starts came home to me in the 1974 America's Cup Trials when I was sailing *Courageous* against *Intrepid, Mariner,* and *Valiant*. It

By being bold at the start, Tom Eamon in Sunfish 14917 got a huge jump. He went on to win.

a

This sequence illustrates mid-line sag and the big hole you can get into by being late. Photo a is prior to the one-minute signal. Photo b was taken with less than one minute remaining. In c the gun has gone, and even in photo d many boats have not yet crossed. By studying the sequence you can

b

c

see how boldness is rewarded (and sometimes punished if you are caught barging, as 707 was). You can also see how certain boats, which looked to be well positioned, lost good spots by chickening out.

d

was soon evident that we were much faster than *Mariner* and *Valiant*, and when starting against them I was abrim with confidence. Throughout the summer I won a higher percentage of the starts against both these boats. Yet against *Intrepid*, which had boat speed comparable to ours, I lost more starts than I won. You could conclude that this only proved that Gerry Driscoll or Bill Buchan, who took turns starting *Intrepid*, were more adept than I. But if you reach this conclusion, then how do you explain the fact that Ted Turner, at the helm of *Mariner*, whom I bested at the majority of the starts, had a better record than Driscoll or Buchan when starting against them? I am convinced it was purely a question of my lack of confidence and lack of sufficient boldness when starting against *Intrepid*.

I've caught myself in similar situations when making fleet starts. I've always prided myself on being a good starter, but every so often I find myself getting a series of mediocre ones. When that occurs, I can often cure it by getting mad at myself and resolving to push more. Almost always my starts will improve, and very seldom do I get over early in the process. By accepting mediocrity you will be mediocre. By pushing for the top you might just get there. Try it and see. I can guarantee that you will do better by that one simple resolve. I can also guarantee that you will never be a good starter, or for that matter a really good sailor, if you don't set your sights high and develop a bold, winning attitude.

The same applies to carrying a spinnaker in heavy going. In the 1963 Trans-Atlantic Race, on *Katama*, we had six straight days of running with the wind always over twenty-five knots, sometimes well over thirty. At first we were a bit apprehensive carrying the spinnaker, especially at night, but since we were racing with an able crew and a good boat, we set it anyway. By the end of the sixth day, we were carrying the chute without incident through some puffs that must have been close to forty knots. I can remember thinking at the time how wonderful it would be to enter a day race in the same boat with the same crew and to hoist the chute in thirty-five knots of wind as soon as we rounded the weather mark. Under such conditions few competitors would set theirs, and our gain would be enormous.

There's a difference, of course, between boldness and lack of seamanship. The time will come when it's blowing too hard to carry spinnaker without danger to the boat, sails or crew. But if you know your capabilities, that time is later rather than sooner.

I recall one race in Solings in which we were carrying our spinnaker on a screaming reach. Although under control, we must have hit twelve knots, judging by the way we planed by the boats sailing under just main and jib. After passing five boats in quick succession, we went into a wild broach, losing two boat places before we could let the chute fly, get back on our feet, retrim the spinnaker, and charge off again, passing more boats before the next broach. We went from twelfth to fifth on that one leg, the only rub being that the boats ahead of us carried their chutes better than we did. One passed us and the other three widened their lead. All but one of the boats that tried to carry spinnaker on that leg (ten in a fleet of thirty-seven) gained by so doing. It was exhilarating, albeit a bit scary. No spinnakers were blown; no boats were damaged. Broaching has to be accepted as an integral part of racing, and those who are determined never to get caught in a broach must resign themselves to mediocrity. It is important to be prudent, vitally important, but it is every bit as important to know when conditions will reward the bold.

Boldness should be shunned, however, whenever it is no longer necessary. After *Constellation* had proven her superiority over *Sovereign* in the first race of the 1964 America's Cup match, we became very conservative. We didn't press at starts, nor did we carry our spinnaker right up to the turning marks. Instead, I would call for a "chicken douse," which meant that I wanted the spinnaker taken down early. The crew didn't particularly like this. They were very competent and would have preferred to show off with a late takedown. But even the most competent crew can get fouled up, a halyard could jam, or some other snafu could develop that might result in a big loss. An early douse will lessen this possibility. Whenever the race is surely won, unless disaster strikes, it's common sense to become conservative and to eschew boldness.

Boldness applies to tactics too. As will be discussed in Chapter 8, it is usually unproductive to cover early in a race. You've got to be bold enough to stick to your guns and to sail your own race, hoping to widen your lead rather than just protect it.

There's an added fillip to being bold on the race course.

You might argue that Brava is being too bold, but she did go on to win the series. Her skipper, John Marshall, explains that this was a day race, with many rescue craft around, and hence they pushed to the limit. They got caught in a windward broach because they were going dead downwind hoping to make the mark and got hit with a forty-knot puff from the lee-

ward quarter. The broach could have been avoided if they had been sailing a bit higher. John avers that in an ocean race with no one around they would have lowered the spinnaker and had a jib winged out instead. There's a time to be bold and a time to be prudent, but never a time to be chicken if you hope to win in keen company.

CARLO BORLENGHI

This sequence in the 1979 J24 Worlds at Newport demonstrates one reason why Jim Scott won. This is the same blow that later crossed the Atlantic to decimate the Fastnet fleet. Scott and his crew carried a spinnaker, hit planing speeds a Twelve Meter could not come close to equaling, lived to tell the tale, and brought home the bacon. Foolhardy? Considering the circumstances and their ability, I don't think so.   J-BOATS

Racing is more fun that way. It becomes even more fun when you find yourself (as you almost certainly will) getting the winning gun more often.

Somewhat akin to boldness is a winning self-image or self-confidence, which all top sailors have. You can't wish yourself into greatness, but, on the other hand, you won't win the big ones unless you feel deep down that you can. I know some sailors who have great boat speed, excellent knowledge, and a full grasp of tactics. They often lead for the first half of a series, but invariably lose it before the end. I suspect that the only thing holding them back is a lack of confidence. They find themselves about to best a sailor of great prominence, and then get so uptight that they wind up beating themselves.

If this happens to you, it might be helpful to realize that the superstar sailor is human too. If you are ahead of him at the halfway point of a race or series, there is no reason why you cannot be there at the end. Just keep sailing in the same fashion, with the same boldness and confidence that got you the lead, and it can do wonders for you. The top sailors do not beat themselves through self-doubt; nor should you.

7

JIBE ON THE LIFTS

It is surprising how many sailors are unaware of the tactic of jibing whenever they are lifted on a run. Many of the good ones who do know about it fail to recognize its vital importance. I came to realize this because quite often when I've mentioned this tactic to good sailors I've received a puzzled look in return, followed by an embarrassed attempt to cover up. But all the really top sailors employ this tactic, and if you hope to join their ranks, it is vital to learn its effectiveness. It is particularly effective in boats that benefit most from tacking downwind, such as scows and catamarans. Could this explain why scow sailors such as Sam Merrick and Buddy Melges are so tough on the run when they switch to keel boats?

Everyone knows that on windward legs it is important to tack in headers, and that it is often better to ignore a minor header if by continuing into it you can get into an even more pronounced one. Jibing in lifts is equally important and usually more effective since so few sailors do it. There is an opportunity for enormous gains.

Upon approaching the windward mark with a run coming up, the first decision is which tack to go on after rounding. Most sailors take the easy way out, choosing the tack that makes for the easier spinnaker set—one that doesn't require a jibe at the mark prior to hoisting the spinnaker. That's a good tactic if you feel the run is a true one and you detect no shifting in the breeze. It's good also if it allows you to start the run on starboard tack, because you will then have right of way over all port tackers still beating for the weather mark.

However, suppose, as you are nearing the mark, you get a pronounced lift on starboard tack. That is the signal to jibe onto port tack before hoisting the chute. You will then be riding a header after rounding, enabling you to head directly for the leeward mark on a fast point of sailing. See figure 8. If the wind is light and you have to keep the boat moving by sailing a bit high of the mark, you will be saving enormous distance on those who are riding a lift on starboard tack and are forced to go much wider of the course to maintain speed.

Once you've settled down at the beginning of a run, check your compass heading. If you feel it is considerably higher of the direct course than that which you could make good on the other tack, you are probably on the wrong tack. You will not be getting to the mark as fast as you could. I say "probably" because, if you anticipate sailing into a greater lift on the tack you are on, it pays to hold on until you get into the lift. But then jibe at once!

The key is to keep looking at the compass. It is far easier to detect lifts and headers on a beat than on a run. They are easier on a beat because most sailors are more aware of their effect. On a run your attention is on the spinnaker and your course is selected (as it should be) to keep the chute drawing effectively to maintain speed. In the process, however, it is all too easy to get so preoccupied that you ignore the compass. You don't realize how much you have been lifted and how far off course you are sailing. The helmsman should keep sailing on the chute, checking the speedometer also, but the tactician should check the compass constantly. As soon as he detects a significant lift, he should so announce and suggest jibing. See figure 9.

This tactic works especially well for still another reason—the reluctance that most sailors have about jibing. Even with a sloppy crew that might muck up the jibe, you will usually lose more by not jibing whenever lifted. Speed is lost every time you jibe, particularly in light air. Still, it is in light air that it becomes particularly important to jibe in the lifts. If you don't, you will sail so far off course to keep speed up that you will wind up

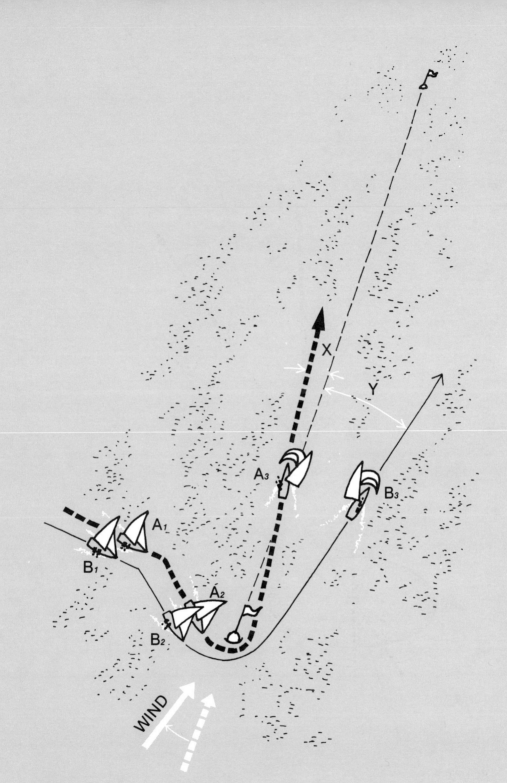

FIGURE 8

The yacht that jibed after rounding is now riding a header toward the leeward mark. She also has kept her wind clear. The starboard tack yacht is sailing a longer course, and will go a lot slower on the dead run.

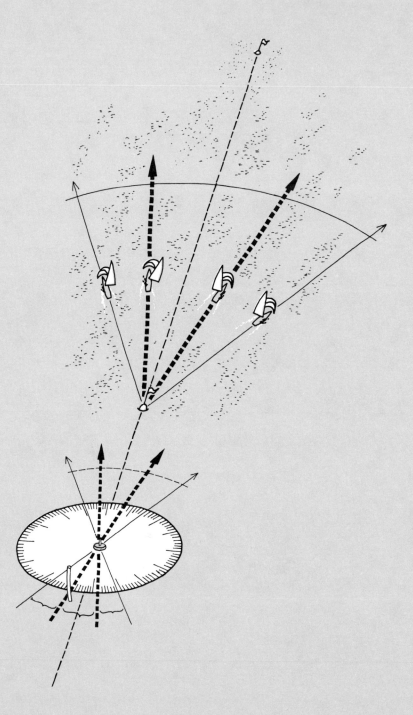

FIGURE 9

The dark arrows on the compass indicate the headings one can steer on a dead run. The exact heading will vary with the wind strength, but the skipper and tactician should determine it at the beginning of the run. If one has to head up to the courses indicated by the light arrows in order to keep the chute full and to maintain speed, then it is well past the time to jibe.

sailing a much greater distance. If the wind shifted back and forth every minute or so, you would lose more through jibing on each lift. However, the wind rarely does shift that often, and the tactic of jibing on every significant lift will almost always pay off.

How do I know how effective this tactic is? Partly by personal experience from instances in which I've gained a great deal by employing it, as well as from other times when I've lost by not. I'm not talking about minor gains or losses, but big ones resulting in a change of five or more positions or hundreds of yards on a single run. I know it works also because I've watched top sailors win big races by using it.

Let's consider a few examples. In 1934 *Rainbow* used it in an America's Cup race to great effect to beat the faster *Endeavour*. The course was leeward-windward, fifteen miles to the leg. *Endeavour* got the start, but *Rainbow*'s spinnaker was set so much faster that she got a good jump. Halfway down the leg, however, *Rainbow*'s spinnaker ripped, and it looked as though *Endeavour* would catch her before another could be hoisted. Mike Vanderbilt noticed, however, that he had been lifted just as the chute was torn. He jibed before setting another one. Thereafter, he had such a better sailing angle that he led at the leeward mark by an astounding four minutes thirty-eight seconds. See figure 10. It's true that J Boats took an eternity to jibe, and that jibing in each lift would have been impractical. But it was true also that ripping a spinnaker and having to replace it was an even greater handicap. This disadvantage was more than offset by the good timing of *Rainbow*'s jibe. *Endeavour* closed on the beat home, but she had already cooked her goose by ignoring this key tactic. Sportswriters were puzzled by how *Rainbow* had suddenly proved so much faster on a run. She wasn't faster—just smarter.

Forty-three years later, *Courageous* won an America's Cup trial race from *Independence* by jibing opportunely. *Independence* was more than a minute ahead starting the run. With a fresh wind blowing, there seemed no way she could be caught since the two boats were virtually even in speed downwind. We on the Selection Committee knew she would keep her wind clear, and signaled for the race to end at the leeward mark. Better to call it there to have time for another race than to send them upwind again so widely separated.

Halfway down the leg, the margin was the same. As *Coura-*

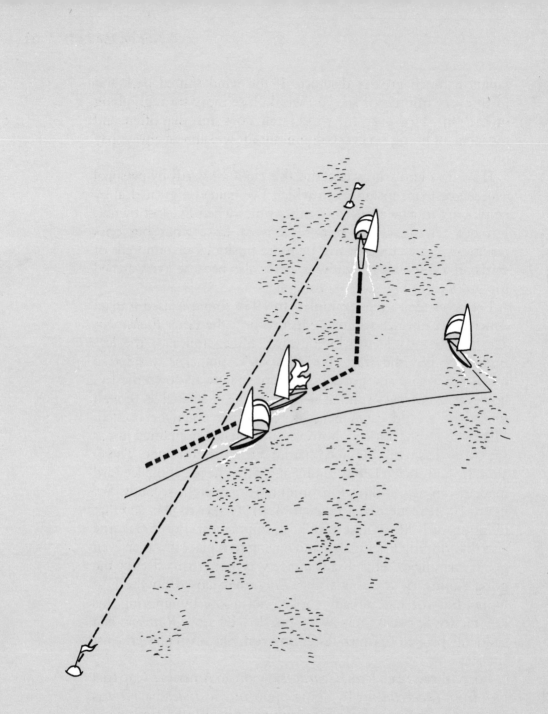

FIGURE 10

When Rainbow *ripped her spinnaker, the wind had just lifted her. Therefore, she jibed before setting a new one and had a good sailing angle for the mark.* Endeavour *was slow in jibing, sailed a longer course (exaggerated here for emphasis) and fell hopelessly behind.*

geous jibed, *Independence* followed suit. This was working fine until, with two-thirds of the leg complete, *Courageous* jibed on a lift; but *Independence* was sufficiently far ahead that when she jibed a moment later the lift had not yet reached her. In a couple of minutes the margin had been halved. When *Courageous* jibed on the next lift, she was close enough so that the leader elected not to jibe for fear of being blanketed. The finish was only a few hundred yards away, and keeping clear air must have seemed like a sure way to stay ahead. The rub was that *Courageous* was now boiling directly for the line while *Independence* was sailing thirty degrees high of it. By the time she did jibe, the lift she had been riding turned into a header. She was now forced to jibe to reach the finish, but on a slower point of sail than *Courageous,* which had again jibed as soon as the header she had been riding turned into a lift. By jibing she retained a faster point of sail. Poor *Independence* had kept her wind clear, but by getting out of phase with the shifts she had maintained slow sailing angles. *Courageous* nipped her right at the line to salvage a race that had seemed lost.

In the third 1970 Cup race, *Intrepid* iced a win against *Gretel II* by pursuing the same tactic, but this time while leading. She was being pursued closely by *Gretel,* and the latter was gaining. *Intrepid* was on her leeward bow with wind just clear. The "book" on match racing would read that she should maintain this position until *Gretel* jibed, and then jibe with her instantly. To do otherwise would violate the match-racing dictum of covering while ahead. But when *Intrepid* got a lift she jibed instantly, away from *Gretel*. *Gretel* seized this opportunity to split with the leader. *Intrepid* was now charging straight for the mark out of sight in the haze ahead, while *Gretel,* on the opposite tack, was sailing at least twenty-five degrees high of it. By the time *Gretel* jibed some five minutes later, a close race had turned into a parade. I cannot believe that Australians didn't know the importance of jibing in a lift, but it appeared that way. They were probably sucked into the course they did sail either by being unsure of the mark's location or by putting more value on splitting with the boat ahead—another real mistake unless you are confident the leader is going the wrong way.

Ten years later, in the second completed America's Cup race, in 1980, *Australia* led *Freedom* at the first four turning marks and there seemed to be no catching her. After rounding the fourth mark with a lead of forty-six seconds, however, it took

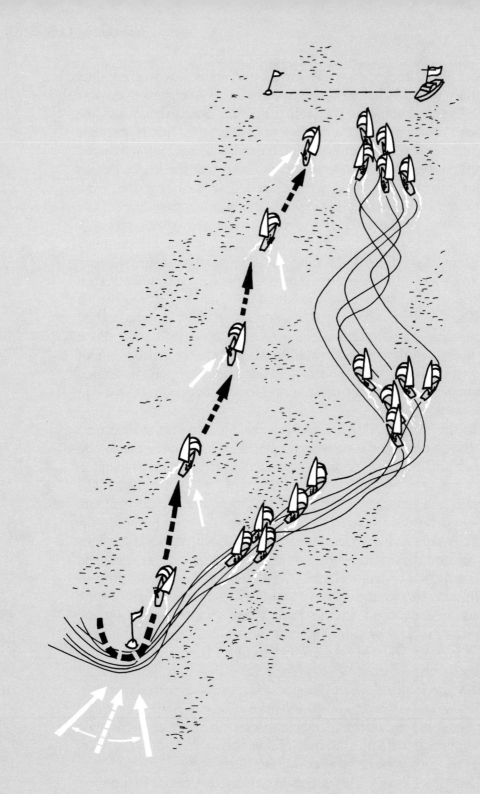

FIGURE 11

By jibing in the lifts as shown by the dark dotted line, while the five boats ahead were fighting each other and hence out of phase, we sailed so much less distance that we came from sixth to second in the Soling Atlantic Coast Championship.

only five minutes of running before *Freedom* had caught her. Here's what happened: *Australia* started downwind on starboard tack, but *Freedom* made a jibe set and went off on port. On *Freedom* they had noticed that the wind had veered just before they reached the mark, which meant that *Australia* was going downwind in a lift. Since *Freedom* jibed, she was riding a header on a much faster sailing angle. *Australia* also had a bit softer air, but it was primarily her failure to jibe immediately when lifted that did her in. Once *Freedom* got the lead the two boats stayed locked together, showing that it wasn't superior boat speed that had enabled *Freedom* to get the lead. *Australia* came from behind to win on the beat to the finish. Had she not done so, this would have been the most important race ever lost through failure to jibe on a lift.

One more example and I trust the point will have been made. A few years ago I was sailing my Soling in the Atlantic Coast championship off Noroton, on Long Island Sound. Rounding the last mark with just a run to the finish, we stood sixth in the fleet of thirty-seven boats. I was rather content to be that well placed in such a tough league, and since the five boats ahead were all good ones and were tightly bunched about a hundred yards ahead of us, there was no realistic hope of catching any of them. It was, however, a puffy northwester with big wind shifts. The five leaders all ran off on starboard tack. We had been lifted on starboard as we approached the mark and set our pole to port. As soon as we had rounded, it was evident we were right as we were headed directly for the mark on a fast point of sail. None of the other five jibed, doubtless because they were so preoccupied with one another. Left all to ourselves, we concentrated on jibing each time we were lifted, making four jibes on the leg to just one or two for the leaders. At the finish we had passed all but one boat with which we were overlapped. See figure 11.

We had been lucky that the leaders had been so tightly bunched that it was harder for them to sail an unmolested course, but otherwise there had been no luck in it. We had no better breeze at any time, but by jibing in lifts we had retained better sailing angles and sailed a shorter distance. If this tactic will work that well in such a tough fleet, think how it can work in the average club outing. The fact is that it will also work surprisingly well against really good boats, as these examples have demonstrated.

8

DON'T COVER EARLY—DO COVER LATE

*M*ost sailors know about covering. Even so, covering becomes a key tactic because it is so often misapplied. It is apt to be given too much importance early in the race and not enough late in the race.

Picture a situation two minutes after the start. If you are fortunate enough to have gotten the jump at the start and have good reason to feel you are on the right tack, *don't* tack when the boats near you do. Chances are they are tacking to clear their wind and will soon be back. If you go with them, you will stay ahead of them, but in the process you will have made two grave errors. First, you will have missed a golden chance to widen your lead on the closest pursuers. Second, the rest of the fleet is apt to have gained by virtue of taking fewer tacks and by getting onto the favored side of the course sooner. Therefore, *never* tack to cover boats near you when the race is young, unless you like the tack they are taking.

If the entire fleet tacks soon after the start and you are leading, the chances are they know something you don't. Even if you prefer the original tack, you'd better flip over pretty soon. But don't rush into tacking. If you really like where you are going you might consider delaying your cover for a short time. Fleets often develop a mass psychology, and when some boats tack just to clear their wind, others are apt to follow suit for no good reason at all.

"But surely this absolute rule of not tacking to cover applies only to fleet racing," you are apt to be thinking. "In a match race, when ahead at the start, you should always tack to cover." Not so, unless you don't like the direction the original tack is taking you. If you do like it, you have a once-in-a-race opportunity to build a small lead into a big one. In match racing the chances are that the two boats will be close at the start, separated usually by less than a length. If you are blanketing or backwinding the boat astern, she has no choice but to tack. But you do have a choice! If you feel you are going the right way and have good reason to feel so by virtue of a better breeze or a favorable shift in the area you are heading toward, you should *not* tack to cover. Under these circumstances the second boat is apt to be compelled to tack back. By now the short lead you have has probably stretched to several lengths and will stretch far more once you do reach the better wind you are heading for. If, however, after the other boat has gone six or seven lengths and shows no sign of tacking back, it would be foolhardy to let her go much farther without covering, unless you would be tacking just short of an obviously better wind.

Courageous employed this tactic with great success in the 1977 America's Cup races. She was ahead at all four starts, but not once did she cover immediately when *Australia* tacked to clear her wind. In each instance *Australia* had to enter the wash from spectator boats. And in each instance *Courageous* got the header she was looking for. Sometimes *Australia* tacked back. Sometimes, after letting her adversary go for seven lengths or so, *Courageous* did flip over to cover. In every case, a mile or so from the start *Courageous* had a commanding lead. She was usually about one minute ahead at the first windward mark and little farther ahead at the finish after twenty additional miles of sailing.

Of course, if you have an early lead and don't like the tack you are on, you should tack immediately when your pursuers tack. In fact, if you can cross them, you should tack *before* they do. The advantage of an early lead is that it gives you the freedom of action to go the way you think is best. This option should not be lost because you feel you should cover. It simply isn't the right time to be conservative. Overprotecting a small lead early in the race, particularly a fleet race, is a pretty sure way to lose it.

An exception to the above does apply in a match race when you are ahead and *know* you have a faster boat. In that instance about the only way you can lose is to let the other boat get away from you. Even the best sailors can, on rare occasions, misread the wind, and there's no sense in taking a risk. When match racing and ahead in a faster boat, tack to cover your adversary, even when you think she is going the wrong way. By so doing, you are apt to win by a smaller margin, but you will surely win.

Timir Pinegin of Russia won a gold medal racing his Star in the 1960 Olympics, largely by following this dictum of not covering early. He got to the Bay of Naples several weeks before the start of the regatta and was out on the race course each day. When the racing started, he had a "book" on where the best winds and shifts were, and he sailed exclusively by the book. He got good starts and never looked back, ignoring the actions of not only his nearest pursuers but also the fleet as a whole. Since his "book" was a good one, he often had big leads at the first mark and was home free.

Bill Ficker employed this tactic of not covering with spectacular success in the America's Cup match against *Gretel II*. He usually was ahead at the start, and he built good leads by sailing his own race and letting *Gretel* go. In this instance he had a compelling reason for doing so because he recognized early that in light-to-moderate air *Gretel* was faster. Hence, he had to follow his judgment and that of his tactician and navigator regarding a fast course, as opposed to observing the more generally accepted tactic of covering when ahead in a match race.

It worked for me, too, in a fleet race for similar reasons. I was racing my Soling in the Atlantic Coast championships. On the first day we managed to survive a whole gale, which sprang up during the race. It blew so hard that less than half the fleet finished. We were relieved to limp home in the fifth spot, but our mainsail had had it. We repaired the torn batten pockets that night, but didn't know until we hoisted the main the next day that it had blown hopelessly out of shape. By then it was too late to go home to get our other main (no beauty but surely better than the one we were forced to use). We had one thing going for us, though. We were sailing on our home waters, and the wind was a shifty northwester. We decided that the only way we would have any chance at all was to sail our own race, hoping the fleet wouldn't follow us. When ahead or well placed early, we never covered unless we felt that that was the only way to go. When behind, we looked for realistic opportunities to split. Following this procedure, we managed to wind up fourth for the regatta with really poor boat speed. I suspect we would not have done as well if we had been going faster. Being slow forced me into never consolidating when ahead because I knew it wouldn't be long before we were caught. I think we were a bit lucky to have things break for us so well, but it did illustrate how effective it can be to throw caution to the wind and, when ahead early, eschew covering for covering's sake.

Does the same apply in distance racing? Most definitely, and, in fact, even more so. In a long race it is fruitless to try to cover a feared competitor except in the very last stages. There are many boats out of your sight that are impossible to cover, and, more importantly, one has to determine what is going to be the fastest course. If you see a hot boat pursuing a different course and especially a boat you would like to cover, there is a psychological reluctance to let her go. However, it is vital to ignore the inclination to cover her. Ruminate on why you think she is going where she is, but don't go with her unless you perceive solid reasons for her course and really prefer her course to the one you had determined was the best. Remember that she could be very wrong. Just over the horizon the bulk of the fleet might very well be going your way, and you may be covering after all. Ocean races are won by long-range planning, which early covering or consolidating can destroy.

We missed winning our class in the 1972 Bermuda Race by failing to practice what I'm preaching here. About 250 miles out from the start we discovered ourselves in the company of much larger boats than our One Tonner, *Witch*. We therefore concluded we were doing very well. We had nearly four hundred miles to go, however, and this was hardly the time to think of consolidating. Still, I succumbed to the temptation. We were farther east than I had ever been before at that stage, some seventy miles east of the rhumb line. I knew that more often than not it paid to be either on the rhumb line or west of it as one neared Bermuda to best take advantage of the prevailing

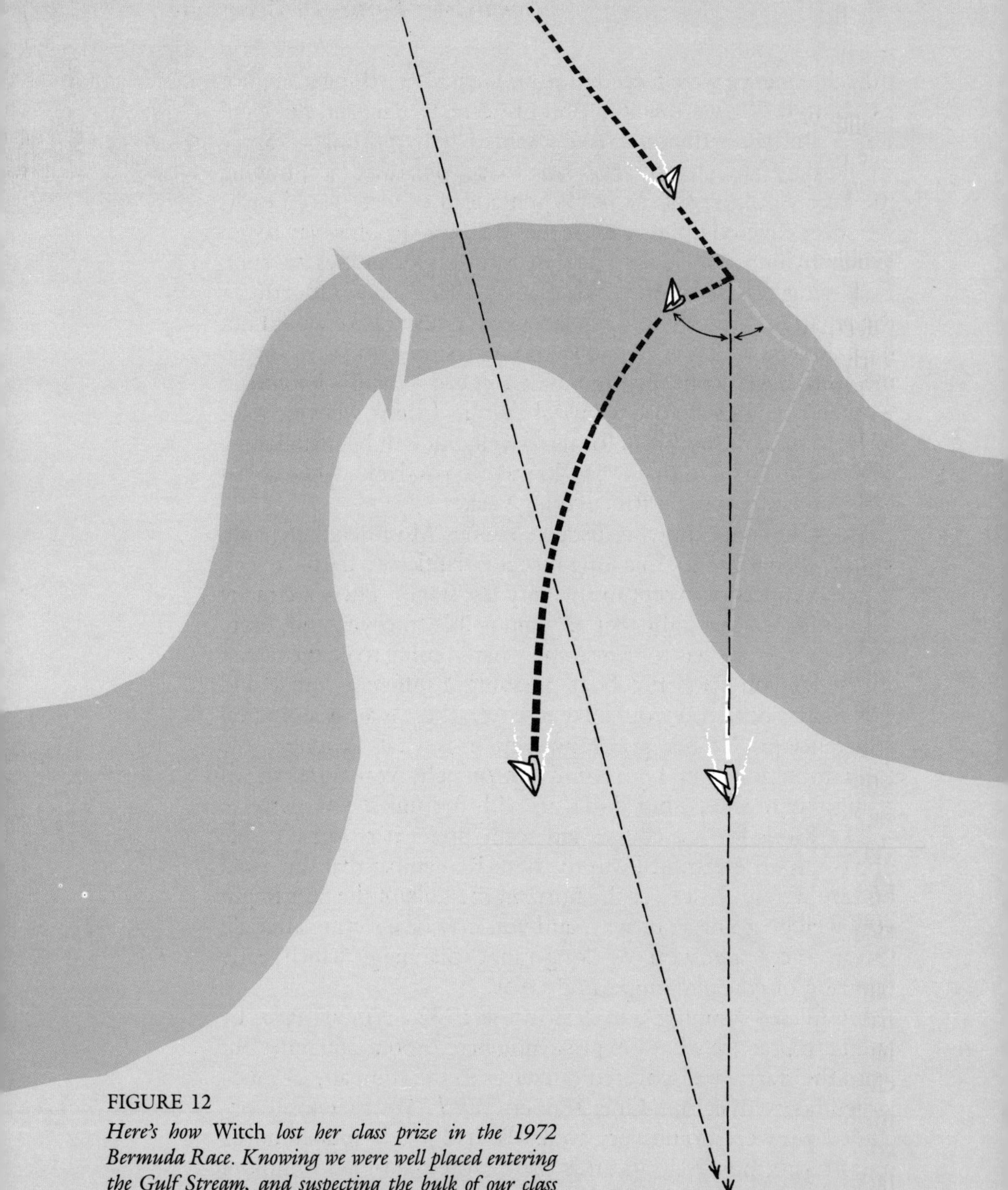

FIGURE 12

Here's how Witch lost her class prize in the 1972
Bermuda Race. Knowing we were well placed entering
the Gulf Stream, and suspecting the bulk of our class
was nearer the rhumb line, we tacked to port to
consolidate. Starboard tack was favored at the time.
When the wind backed an hour after we tacked, the
distance sailed in the preceding hour just put us to
leeward and was thrown away. We had been stupid in
"covering" with four hundred miles to go instead of
continuing to ride the current on the tack that took us
closer to Bermuda.

southwester. I concluded that the bulk of the fleet, knowing this also, was probably west of us at this stage. Since we appeared to be very well placed, it seemed wise to consolidate our good position by getting a bit farther west. I was apprehensive about this, however, because starboard tack, which would take us still farther east, was within thirty degrees of fetching the island, whereas on port tack we would be fifty-five degrees off course. Moreover, starboard tack would enable us best to ride the Gulf Stream current. It all added up to being the right way to go even though it would take us still farther east. I decided, however, to compromise, tacking onto port tack for one hour to do just a bit of consolidating of our presumed good position and then tacking back onto starboard. It was one of the worst decisions I have ever made. At the end of our hour's tack on port, we were lifted twenty degrees and we kept getting lifted. It was impossible to tack back, and for the next two days we were hard on the wind on port tack, but still not fetching Bermuda. If, instead of tacking to port "for one hour," we had held starboard tack, flipping over only when port tack took us closer to Bermuda, we would have saved several miles. Our tack to port had succeeded only in getting us to leeward. We failed to win our class by two minutes thirty-seven seconds and must have lost at least fifty minutes by tacking to port when we did. I deserved this fate because I had violated a basic tactic for covering and consolidating early in the race. With nearly four hundred miles to go, it was far more important to continue sailing a course that showed more promise rather than the more conservative one I elected. See figure 12.

There is, however, a tactic that I like to refer to as a compromise cover that does make sense in the early stages of a race. Say you have an early lead, are going the way you think is best, and to your surprise the bulk of the fleet goes off on the other tack. Then it makes sense to cover them part way, favoring the side of the course you think is best but not going for broke. See figure 13. You might lose a boat or two that does go for broke sailing right to the layline on the side of the course you thought best but that the majority of the fleet avoided. But you also will avoid the danger of a real dumping if the bulk of the fleet turns out to be right and you are wrong in determining the favored side of the course. And if you are right you will still have a big jump on the fleet as a whole, and since the race is still relatively young you might still be able to overtake the boat that sailed a more reckless course well off to one side. In a big fleet, series are usually won by more consistent high finishers than by a combination of first and poor finishers.

But Do Cover Late

Although it is foolish to cover or to consolidate too much early in a race, it is even worse *not* to do so in the later stages. If you have comfortable lead on the last leg of a race with a prime rival close astern, it is plain common sense to cover, even if you suspect that the boat astern is going the wrong way. You could be wrong, and, even if right, you can afford to lose a bit of distance to be certain of staying ahead of the boat or boats close astern. If it's fluky, however, keep a watchful eye on boats farther back to be sure that you don't get so carried away with covering the nearest pursuers that you let the pack through. That's not apt to happen because there's not much of the race left for it to happen in. Still, you should guard against it by being alert.

The problem becomes more difficult if you have two close pursuers who have split tacks with each other. Say with half a mile to go you have a fifty-yard lead on the second boat and a seventy-five-yard edge on the third. It is then smarter to cover the third boat if you think she is going the right way. The second boat may be so anxious to take first place that she takes a flyer, going the way she feels is wrong in the hopes that you won't cover her and with the further hope that the "wrong" way turns out to be right after all. Don't get sucked into this ploy. If you do, the boat in third place is very apt to wind up winning, with you second and the boat that was second in the third spot or worse. Cover the nearest pursuer only if you like where she is going, or if you have no preference as to which tack is better. It goes without saying that, if the nearest boat is the one you must beat to win a series and you are sailing the final race, then you must cover her willy-nilly, provided no other boat can take the series if you lose several places.

In match racing it becomes doubly important to cover your pursuer late in the race, and, in fact, quite early in the race if you have built a comfortable lead and have equal boat speed.

In the 1977 America's Cup trials, Lowell North in *Enterprise* lost several races by ignoring this key tactic. One race against *Courageous* illustrated the point particularly well. When *Enterprise* rounded the leeward mark with but a single beat to the

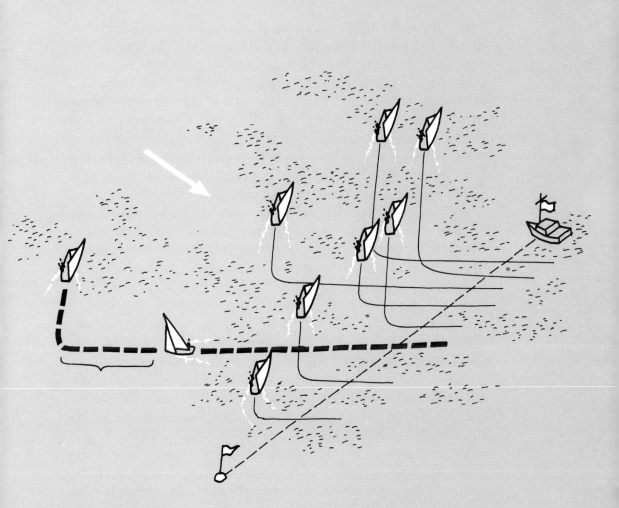

FIGURE 13

The dotted line shows what I like to term a "compromise cover." You've taken the start, you like the left side of the course, and therefore even though the fleet tacks to port you don't tack with them immediately. Instead, by delaying your tack, you are protecting the left side of the course and have a chance to gain a big lead. Since you are a prudent skipper, you do tack eventually instead of going for broke. You've made a compromise cover and have hedged your bets.

finish, she had a ten-length lead. Throughout the race her boat speed had been at least equal, and it appeared there was no way *Enterprise* could lose. Lowell found the way. There was a seven-knot wind blowing from the southeast. To the south you could see better wind, while to the east it was flat. *Enterprise* quite rightly went off on port tack, but when *Courageous* tacked toward the east on starboard side, she failed to cover. I remember discussing this at the time with others on the Selection Committee. We all agreed that, although *Enterprise* was almost certainly sailing the faster course, even more certainly she was doing the only thing that gave *Courageous* any chance at all. For the first mile *Enterprise* widened her lead to about three times what it had been at the mark. As she neared the line of breeze she had been heading for, it started to diminish. To make matters worse she started getting lifted, making it difficult to tack to cover. *Courageous* was still light too, and for a while it looked as though *Enterprise* would hold her lead. Then we saw a new wind building to the east, and *Courageous,* though still behind, was closer to it. *Enterprise* did tack at this juncture, but on an unfavorable slant. *Courageous* was now nearer the new wind. She got it first and won the race by over a mile! Lowell was so certain his course was right that he overlooked the most basic of all key tactics: covering in the later stages.

Turner never made this mistake. That's one reason why in the match against *Australia,* after gaining a comfortable lead, he seldom widened it much. He covered *Australia* relentlessly no matter where she went. He thereby lost opportunities to get still farther ahead, but insured that there was no way to lose the race. A one-minute victory after twenty-four miles of sailing counts just as much as winning by ten minutes.

Intrepid lost one race to *Gretel II* in the 1970 America's Cup match, and did it by ignoring this tactic. *Intrepid* at least had some excuse. By not covering, she had built a lead on *Gretel II* in weather that favored *Gretel*. In light air she could not tack with *Gretel,* and, when ahead, she avoided tacking duels. Instead, she let *Gretel* go whenever she felt *Gretel* was flipping onto the wrong tack. This tactic had built a lead of over a minute with but one beat remaining. With a lead of that magnitude and only one weather leg to the finish, it was time to switch tactics. It was a long and a short tack to the finish, and *Intrepid* quite rightly took the long one. You could visualize their thinking. A header would put them still farther ahead. A lift would enable them to fetch, or nearly so. It all added up, except for one thing. With a lead of over a minute, they had a sufficient margin to cover *Gretel,* lose something in the process, but still retain enough of a lead to win. Instead, when *Gretel* tacked away, they let her go. *Gretel* sailed into a header, tacked on it, and was fetching the finish. *Intrepid* could have tacked at this instant, and then tacked back in a safe leeward position for a narrow victory. But she hesitated for a few minutes, and, when she did tack, it was too late. *Gretel* crossed her and went on to win by over a minute. It was one of the few mistakes Bill Ficker, his tactician, Steve Van Dyck, and navigator, Peter Wilson, made in the entire series. They had become mesmerized by their earlier success through not covering. They had overlooked the fact that in this situation, with a comfortable lead, they should have reversed these tactics in favor of the safer and surer one of covering late in the race when they had a sizable lead. I talked with Ficker, Van Dyck, and Wilson right after the race. Before I had a chance to say anything, they admitted that they had blown it. It was one of the first and last mistakes they were to make in the match, but it was a doozy.

Perhaps the point has been made already, but I would like to tell you about one instance of not covering late that worked, but may well have hurt the winning skipper forevermore. I told you about Russia's Timir Pinegin winning the Star Olympics in 1960 by ignoring the fleet early in the race and building big leads. The astounding part was that after getting well out in front he continued to sail his own race. Often on the first beat he would get well ahead by going off on port tack. Then, on the last beat, with the fleet going off on port tack, Pinegin would go his merry way on starboard and double his lead. He had the weather pattern so well calculated and was so confident that he sailed his own race rather than protecting large leads late in the race. I was there as a member of the International Jury, which gave me a ringside seat. I was full of admiration for Pinegin's forecasting and his courage. There's no question that he deserved the gold medal. Still, at the time I predicted that he would never win another big championship. I based this on the fact that in keen competition no one was so infallible that he could continue to violate the key tactic of covering late in a race and be successful. Pinegin has not won a big championship since the glorious series he pulled off in 1960.

9

DON'T BE
A SHEEP
(BUT DO PURSUE)

*Y*achting magazine's editor, Bill Robinson, didn't have a chance. He was the skipper of the Bermuda 40 *Jaan* in the 1971 S.O.R.C. Lipton Cup race. His crew was composed of family and friends, as opposed to the young gorillas manning most of the boats in this grand prix ocean-racing event. To make matters still more hopeless, he was sailing a boat that was outclassed by the flat-out ocean racers that made up the bulk of the fleet. Bermuda 40s are lovely boats and have earned their reputation as classics. They are fast cruising boats, but the word *cruising* is the catch when pitted against an S.O.R.C. fleet. True, *Jaan* did have the optional tall rig, but she also had air conditioning, a water maker, deep freeze, shower, extra tankage, and every creature comfort to make her a superb cruising boat. Entering her in this race was akin to competing in the Le Mans twenty-four-hour sports-car race with a Rolls Royce sedan.

"What the hell," said Bill. "It's a beautiful day, we have a good navigator, and it will be more fun entering the race than following it as a spectator. And if we have enough reaching, we might get as high as the middle of our class."

The course was a broad spinnaker reach from Miami to a mark boat a couple of miles past Sunny Isle buoy, near Fort Lauderdale, followed by a beat home. A decision had to be made whether to head well offshore to pick up the favorable Gulf Stream current or to sail a shorter rhumb-line course in slack water. Since the mark boat was so close to the beach, Bill and his navigator, Jim Davis, opted for sailing the short course, despite the fact that almost all of the Class A, B, and C boats, which had started earlier, were heading well offshore. When Class D started, all of them charged off after the boats ahead, all, that is, except *Jaan*. On *Jaan* they just didn't believe that current would offset the extra distance.

As the morning wore on, however, Bill became anxious. It is difficult when in a parade and out of step with everyone else to believe that you are the only one in step. Jim Davis stuck to his guns. Both Bill and he became puzzled when their running fixes showed them to be only two miles from the turning point and there were no boats on the return leg, even the seventy-three footers, which had started well ahead. Instead, the fleet was milling about in many different and apparently aimless directions. "What are they doing?" Bill asked Jim. "Damned if I know," he answered, "but we're heading right for the mark boat, and it isn't far away." A few minutes later they spied it through binoculars. She was nestled among a number of fishing boats, which made her hard to spot. The truth was that all of Classes A, B, and C had overshot it, and the other Class D boats were much too far offshore. See figure 14.

By this time the Class A boats had realized their error and were heading back for the mark. Still, most of the fleet kept following blindly toward where the others had been before doubling back. It was a delightful moment as *Jaan* rounded in the middle of Class A and B. She started home a full mile ahead of the next boat in her class. The beat home wasn't to her liking, but by virtue of not having followed blindly on the way out, *Jaan* managed to finish first in her class, both on corrected time and boat for boat.

This is the most extreme example I have ever encountered of a whole fleet, save one, playing follow the leader when the leaders were going very much astray. Although this is the all-time classic case, it is far from unique.

There is something in human nature that makes it very difficult to avoid being a sheep, something that makes even good

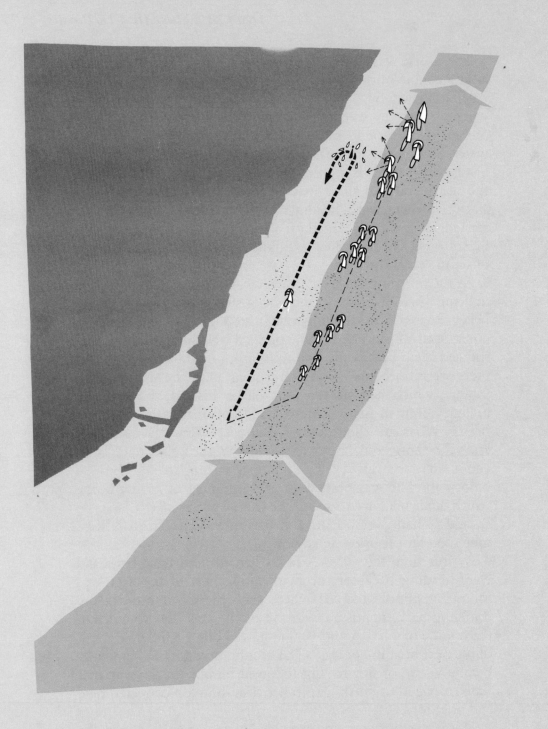

FIGURE 14

Jaan's course is shown by the heavy dotted line. It often works to sail the longer course by going offshore into the favorable Gulf Stream current, but not if you fail to find the mark and overshoot it. By not being a sheep and sticking to her guns while the fleet ahead swept well past the mark, Jaan scored a big win.

sailors conclude that the boats up ahead must be going the right way. If the hot skippers in your class are going a certain way, it takes real guts not to follow. It's all too easy to follow them basing that judgment on the conclusion that they must know what they are doing. It is not uncommon to get swept up in a mass psychology and to stop thinking for yourself. If you've raced a good deal, I am sure you can remember instances when the lead boat headed for the wrong mark, or left it on the improper side, and became a Pied Piper, drawing a number of other boats into the same error.

A less flagrant, more subtle, but also more prevalent example is the tendency to follow the skippers with the best reputation onto whichever tack they may choose on a windward leg. More often than not, the good skippers *are* going the right way; but even the best of them get screwed up on occasion. After analyzing the situation, if the tack the hotshots are taking doesn't make sense to you, have the courage to split. Often the early leader isn't at all sure which way to go, but if he finds the bulk of the fleet following, he has no reason to tack. By maintaining his tack he is covering, and should he go about, only some of the fleet will tack with him. If you are a sheep and follow him, you only make his job easier and give yourself little chance of passing.

One sees this same mass psychology in the early stages of a long-distance race. In the Bermuda Race, for example, if the prevailing southwesterly is blowing, making it a bare fetch for the island over six-hundred miles away, you will see most of the boats hard on the wind to remain on the rhumb line. In so doing, they will lose perhaps half a knot of speed to the few boats that ease off to head several degrees lower. A few hours later the wind will almost certainly have shifted. If it frees, the boats that drove off at high speed will be lifted up to course. If it heads, they will be able, should they so desire, to tack, crossing the boats that went hard on the wind at the outset. Yet in such circumstances you will find most of the fleet holding high, hewing to the rhumb line, but because their speed is reduced, not closing the finish as fast as the few boats that drove off at higher speed. I suspect few sailors would hold so high if they were sailing out of sight of competitors. When you see boats on your quarter holding up, it's difficult not to be sucked up with them. Pretty soon almost everyone is doing it—everyone, that is, except for a few smart skippers who learned long ago the folly

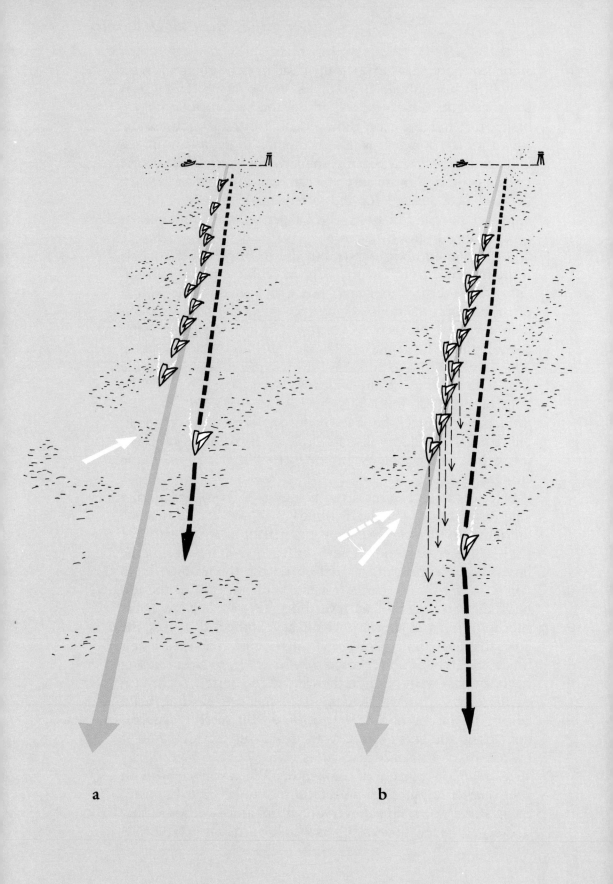

a   b

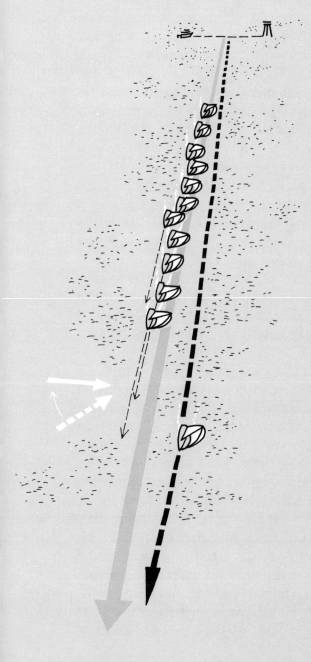

c

FIGURE 15

At the start of the Bermuda Race, if you can just fetch the island, the bulk of the fleet will go hard on the wind to stay on the rhumb line. The smart skipper will foot off a bit at high speed, as shown by the dotted line (a). The wind is almost sure to head or lift the fleet. If it heads, the boat that has driven off will find the fleet (now far behind) falling into his wake (b). If the wind hauls to produce a lift, then the boat that was to leeward can now fetch the island, and having sailed faster before being lifted, is once again well out in front (c). This basic tactic is overlooked with surprising frequency.

of becoming a sheep. Thinking for yourself is a key way to win races. See figures 15a, b, and c.

You are not being a sheep if you follow boats ahead that you feel are going the right way. In fact it's an even greater error to split with them just for the sake of splitting in the hopes for a break that will let you gain. Particularly if the race is young and you are doing poorly, it is vital to follow the fleet just as long as you feel they are going the right way. It will be discouraging, but it's better than taking a different course that is based on wishful thinking. Should you split in such instances, the chances are you will just fall farther behind and hopelessly out of the race. By pursuing you will remain in close enough contact to be able to take advantage of later opportunities.

It is apt to rattle the leader if he finds you always on his heels in close pursuit, ready to pounce on his first mistake. In a significant final trials race in 1964, we on *Constellation* finally passed *American Eagle* by this very tactic. For eighteen miles we sailed within several lengths of *American Eagle,* tacking to clear our wind but never attempting to split. This enabled us to keep close. When Bill Cox started tacking too fast during a tacking duel on the last leg, we were able to get by. If we had not stayed close, waiting for him to make a mistake, we would never have been able to capitalize.

Failure to pursue cost me a chance to gain the Sears Cup finals in 1936. I had won the first three races, and, in the fourth, had what I felt was a perfect start. Since I was adjacent to the starting buoy, I was sure I was not early at the start, and I did not return immediately when my number was called for a premature start. When it was called several more times, I did return, only to be informed that the man on the line had called the wrong number (because of mirror vision he had read 47 as 74, recalling me by mistake). By this time the fleet was long gone. I decided my only way to pick up any boats was to go off on a flyer by myself. This just put me hopelessly behind. I had a fast boat, and, had I pursued the fleet instead of splitting, I am confident I would have passed at least one boat, and that's all I would have needed to win the series. The series winner went on to win the Sears Cup finals, which made my failure to pursue even harder to swallow.

There's another advantage in pursuing just as long as you feel the course of the leader is correct. Many skippers don't have the persistence to stick it out and will tack away in hopes of a break.

Such fliers seldom pay off, and the skippers who do tack away are usually passed by those with more patience. Relentless pursuit is a far cry from being a sheep, and, if you have good boat speed, you might even go on to win.

If *Gretel II* had pursued *Intrepid* in the 1970 America's Cup match, her superior light-air speed might well have enabled her to win. Instead, she got hopelessly behind when she tacked away and *Intrepid* let her go.

By thinking for yourself, it's easy to tell the difference between blind following and relentless pursuit. By so doing, you will do better on the race course.

10

ANTICIPATE

I can think of no key to successful racing more important
than anticipation. The best skippers, while concentrating on the
immediate situation, still focus more than half of their thinking
well into the future. They think less about what's happening
now and more about what is apt to happen later. In a day race
"later" could be ten minutes into the future. In an ocean race it
could be a number of hours or even a day or more ahead. In
either case, position yourself into the most advantageous spot
for the future as opposed to the present situation.

Quite often anticipation is so simple as to be laughable. I can
absolutely guarantee that, in a start with a strong favorable
current setting you up to the line, the vast majority of the fleet
will be early, killing speed just prior to the start to avoid being
over early. Armed with that knowledge, the sharp skipper will
hold back in the certainty that, as the final countdown occurs, he
can sheet in and charge for the line, sweeping past the bulk of
the fleet, which is stalled out. See figures 16a and b. This sounds
basic, but believe me, it will happen every time. The reverse is
true when starting against a strong head current. That's the time
to crowd it, to go for broke, because almost everyone will be

late. It also has the advantage of minimum risks; if you overdo it and are early, you can get back to restart without too great a loss. In a strong foul current it is often possible to get away with barging. See figures 17a and b.

I well remember one Fastnet race, a windward start with a strong favorable current and light air. True to form, the bulk of the fleet was too close to the line and had to kill time. We on Bob Derecktor's *Salty Goose,* hanging below the pack, were able to sweep past in the last few seconds into a commanding early lead. By maintaining high speed well short of the line we could if necessary have dipped down against the current, thus removing the possibility of being over early with its disastrous consequences. Two boats, despite frantic last-minute efforts to hold back, were swept over early. Even though they set spinnakers to return, it was *three hours* before they could get back to the line to restart. By this time we were out of sight. One of the early starters came within an hour of winning this premier ocean race. They must have anticipated everything else in the days ahead far better than they did at the start.

Failure to anticipate current can, and often does, have disastrous results at turning marks. When beating to a windward mark against a strong current, you can be sure that a number of boats will tack too short and hit the mark. The famed boating photographer Morris Rosenfeld realized this and often positioned himself at the windward mark whenever there was a strong head current. He got some great shots of boats and sails draped all over the mark.

Anticipation begins, quite properly, before the start. When one end of the starting line is favored (either by being cocked closer to the wind, closer to the first mark, or nearer to an anticipated beneficial windshift), you can be sure that the bulk of the fleet will be there. The accompanying diagrams illustrate what I mean by favored end. See figures 18, 19, 20, and 21.

If you feel confident that you can get the number-one start at that end, then go for broke and try for it. But in keen competition, the odds are against it. Only one boat can be ahead of the crowd, and if you aren't that boat you will be in a real mess. Therefore, in a sharp fleet it's better not to join the crowd at the favored end. Instead, make your approach a bit to windward of the leeward end when it is favored, and a bit to leeward of the windward end when it is. Concentrate on getting clear air. In each instance one boat will be ahead of you at the start, but the

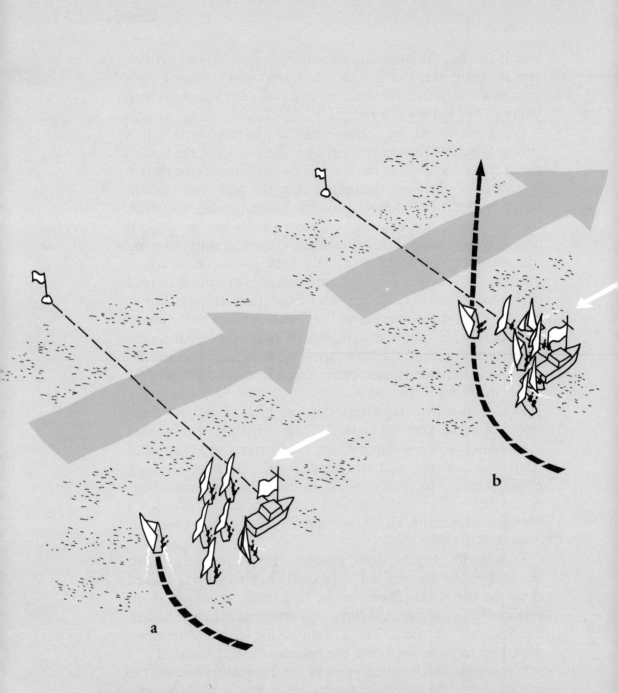

FIGURE 16

In a strong fair current, many boats will be stalling to keep from being swept over the line before the gun. Some are apt to be early. That's the time to lay back and charge through with full headway, as shown. In this instance a safe course is apt to result in the best start of all.

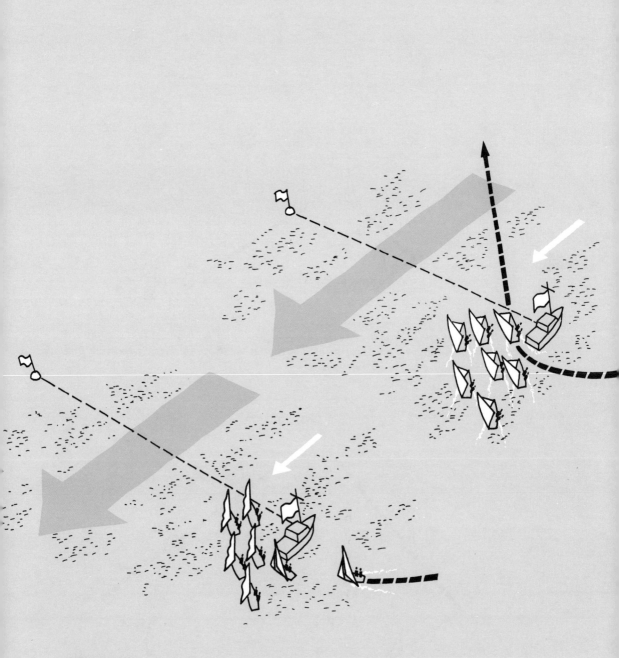

FIGURE 17

With a strong head current, it is often possible to get a fine start by barging. Boats clustered by the committee boat waiting for time to run out will be swept to leeward by the current and a gap will almost invariably open. Remember that barging is perfectly legal if there is room.

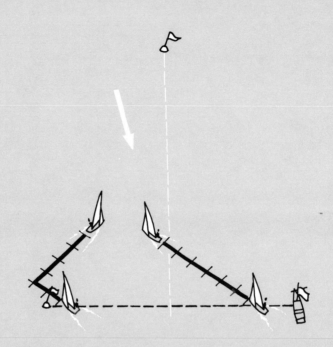

FIGURE 18

Here the leeward end is favored since the line is perpendicular to the course to the windward mark, instead of being square to the wind. The boat at the buoy can therefore tack and cross the boat that started at the committee boat.

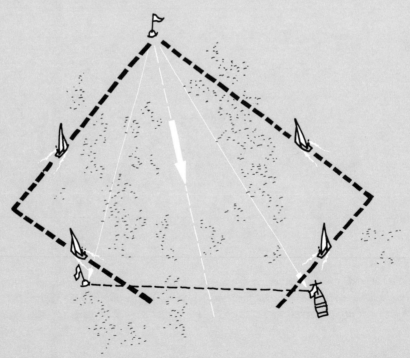

FIGURE 19

If the wind holds steady, the advantage gained by starting at the favored leeward end of the line will prevail to the mark.

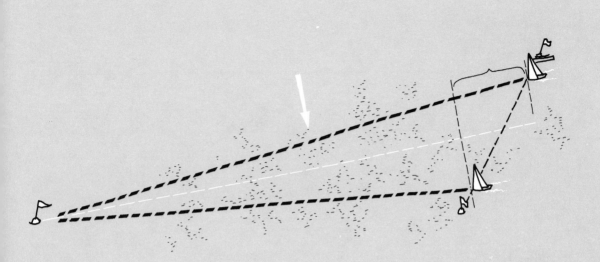

FIGURE 20

On a reaching start, which is common on port-to-port runs or distance races, the leeward end is often closer to the mark. Even if just a little closer, it is a safe place to start since the apparent wind is forward of the true wind, and the chances of being blanketed are nil. The smart skippers get an early jump by being at that end, and the jump is accentuated by the fact that the bulk of the fleet will start at the windward end.

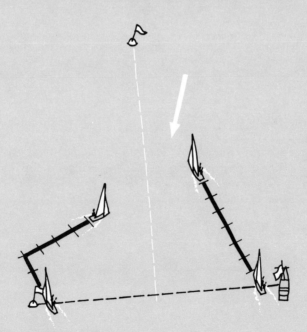

FIGURE 21

In this instance, the windward end is so favored that the boat at the committee-boat end has a huge jump.

FIGURE 22

With the leeward end of the line favored, but with a wind shift anticipated on the right side of the course, a port tack start can prove productive. Even if you duck some starboard tack boats you will cross those at the "wrong" end of the line and will be first into the header.

boats at the favored end will hurt each other sufficiently so that you will soon be in second place. And early second in a fleet race is not a bad place to be. Figure 5 in Chapter 5 illustrates this start.

If you anticipate that the favored side of the course is to the right (favored because there is better wind, less adverse current, or a beneficial wind shift expected on that side), it is more important to avoid starting at the extreme leeward end of the line even if favored. Even though you get the start at that end, it might be a couple of minutes before you can tack onto port and clear boats that started on your weather quarter. This is the time to consider a port-tack start, even though you might have to dip a number of starboard tackers. See figure 22. You may also consider starting a bit late at the "wrong" end, the windward end, of the line so that you can be sure of being able to move immediately onto port tack. See figure 23. If the right side is as much favored as you anticipate, you might very well be in the lead several minutes after the start even though you crossed the line on the "wrong" end. It's important to realize that the boat that really got the start is the one that is on top several minutes after the gun, not the one in the lead as the gun sounds.

What if the windward end is favored, and the right side of the course is also expected to be the way to go? That's the time to consider a late start at the windward end of the line. The only reason to be late is the pragmatic one of insuring that you have the ability to tack at will. Sure, it would be better still to get the start at the weather end, but suppose you are a bit early and have to drive off at the last moment? There is then no way you can tack and cross the slightly late starter at the favored end. What usually happens is that the late starter moves onto port tack as soon as she crosses. The number-one starter tacks with her, but not on her wind. The boat with the "second best" start at the favored end has to keep sailing on starboard tack so long that by the time she can tack over she is well behind the boat that was purposely late at the favored end. See again figure 23.

With the left side of the course favored, going for broke at the leeward end of the line assumes greater importance, especially if it is the favored end. Even if you fail to get the start, and even if you have to eat dirty air, at least you are going the right way. Eventually you will get your wind clear. Though not in the lead, you will be well positioned, within striking distance of the boat or boats (very few) ahead of you in the early stages of the race.

With windward end favored there is sure to be a crowd at that end of the line. The black sloop just made it without barging. Numbers 3566 and 2601 have safer starts, especially if they have good headway. Number 4747 is barging and may or may not get away with it. But it wasn't worth the risk.

There's no excuse for this group of bargers at a Bermuda Race start. Many could be protested, all are blanketed by the committee boat, and the leeward end, with clear air, is favored. Still, in distance races one can anticipate a crowd at the windward end of the line. Therefore, start down the line, way down if the leeward end is favored.

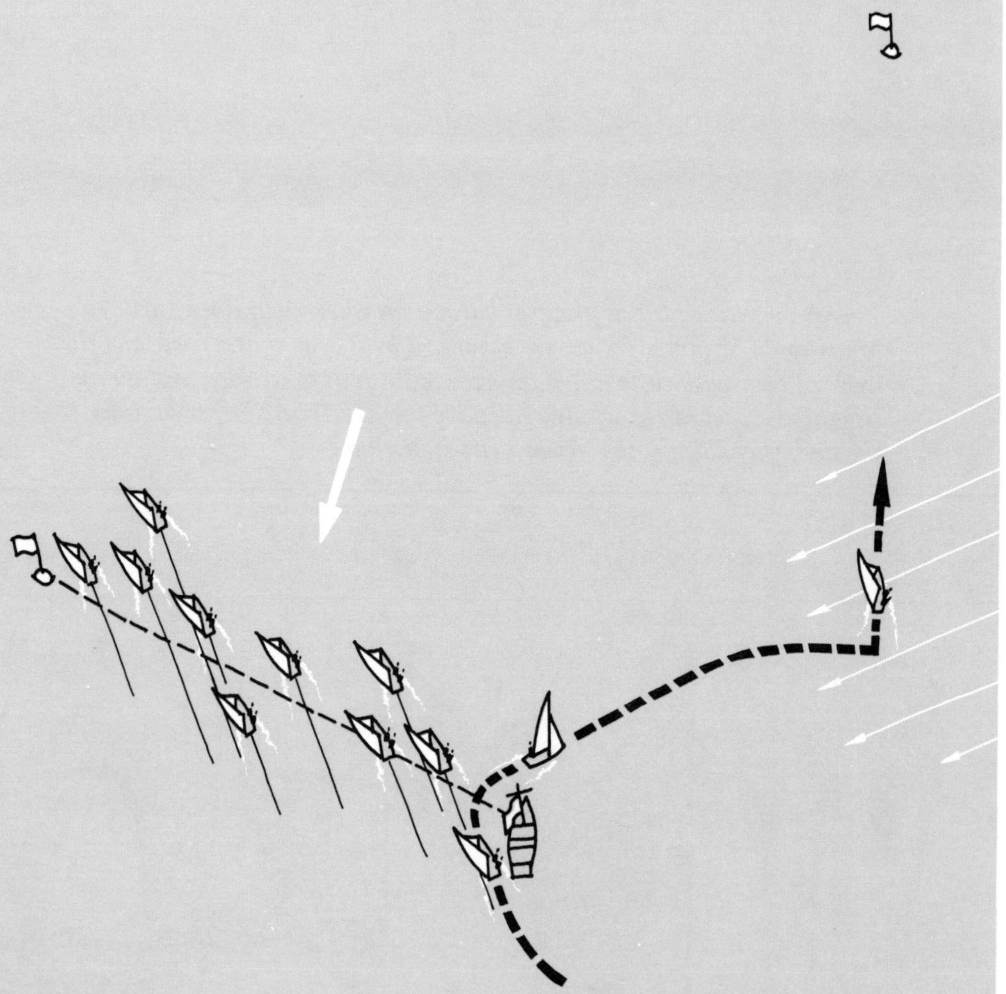

FIGURE 23

Even though late at the windward end, by tacking first into the anticipated header, you can be leading soon after the start.

It's satisfying to be leading a few minutes after the start. In a sizable fleet, however, it is much more important to insure that you are close to the leaders and able to go in the direction you feel is favored. Proper anticipation will get you there almost every time.

Anticipation at the start is equally important in a match race. Dennis Conner demonstrated this fact in the 1980 America's Cup match against *Australia*. In all five races he positioned *Freedom* at the start so that he could be sure of going on the first beat to the side of the course that he expected to be favored. In both the first and third races this enabled him to gain commanding leads against a boat that was faster in the light air that prevailed. Thereafter, he found it easy to stay on top by protecting the favored side of the course. If Jim Hardy, sailing *Australia,* had anticipated as well and governed his starting tactics accordingly, he could very possibly have won the first three races. He proved his boat speed by winning the second race. In the fourth and fifth races Conner also anticipated well, and since *Freedom* was faster in the winds dished up for those contests, he won both these races by margins far greater than those that would have been provided by the difference in boat speed alone.

Secondary opportunities for either major gains or losses in a fleet race occur at turning marks. In a close race with a bunched fleet, being the outside boat rounding a mark can cost you several places. The time to avoid this dire circumstance is well before arriving at the mark. Assume you are two hundred yards from the mark with three boats overlapping you on the inside. It's easy to anticipate that this is a no-win situation if allowed to continue. What to do? There are two options. You can kill speed, drop astern of the three boats inside of you, and then sharpen up in hopes of gaining an inside overlap on all of them, rounding perhaps second of the group instead of fourth. See figure 24. Or you can drive off to leeward in the expectation that the other three will start fighting each other, heading up to gain the inside berth at the turn. If they do it enough and get sufficiently high, you might well be able to reach through their lee at the end, breaking the overlap and rounding first or second. See figure 25. If at the last minute you see that neither of these options is going to work, then instead of being caught on the outside of four boats rounding together, it is wise to drop astern of the other three, approach the mark wide, and sharpen up to take it close aboard when on the next leg's course, following

JACK KNIGHT

This FD start proves the great talent in this class. Numbers E217 and US1122 have great starts at the leeward end (US1122 better have full headway to avoid being run over). But what impresses me most are the fine starts made by a few boats in the middle of the line. They knew about mid-line sag and thereby got a jump on the pack without being over early.

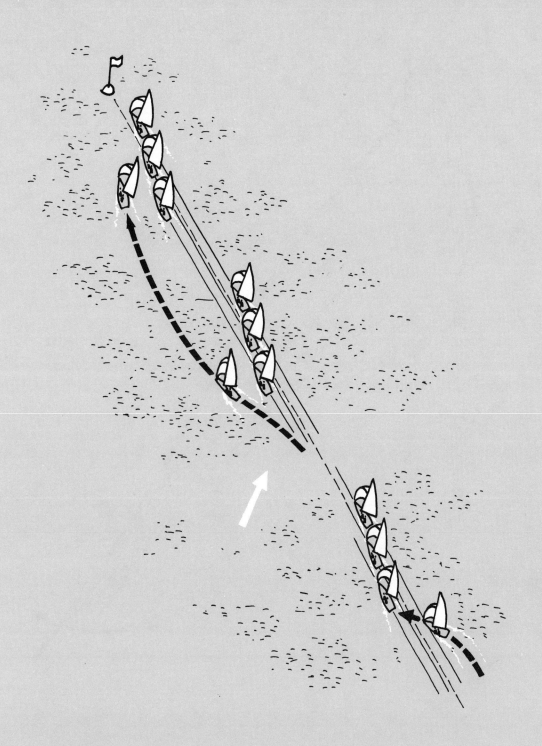

FIGURE 24

The fourth boat, noting that the boats ahead are not sailing high, sharpens up, thereby gaining speed and an overlap on all but the lead boat, rounding second instead of fourth.

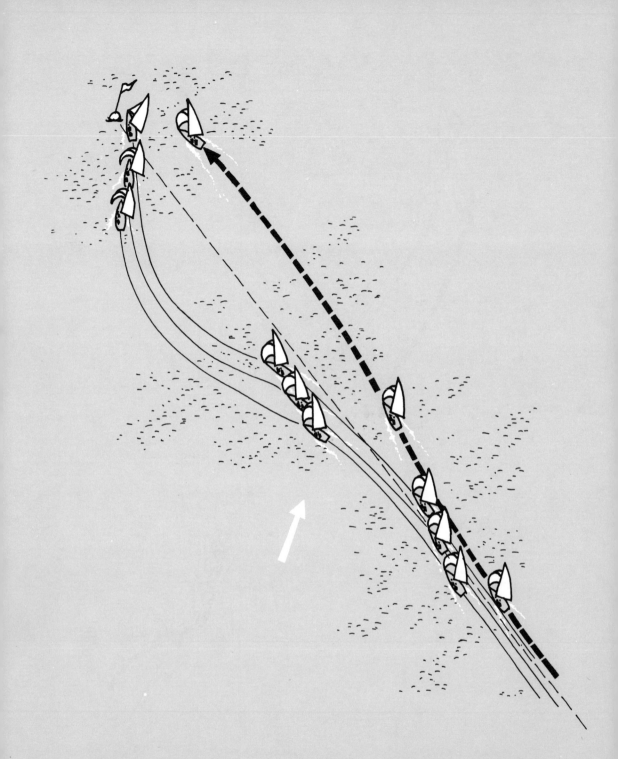

FIGURE 25

When the fourth boat notes the three boats ahead of her sharpening up to fight for an overlap, she drives off to leeward. When the leaders slow down as they square off for the mark, she charges through to leeward on a fast point of sail, rounding second. This tactic, and the one shown in figure 24, can sometimes result in rounding first. Although neither tactic always works, it is better to try rather than to settle for fourth.

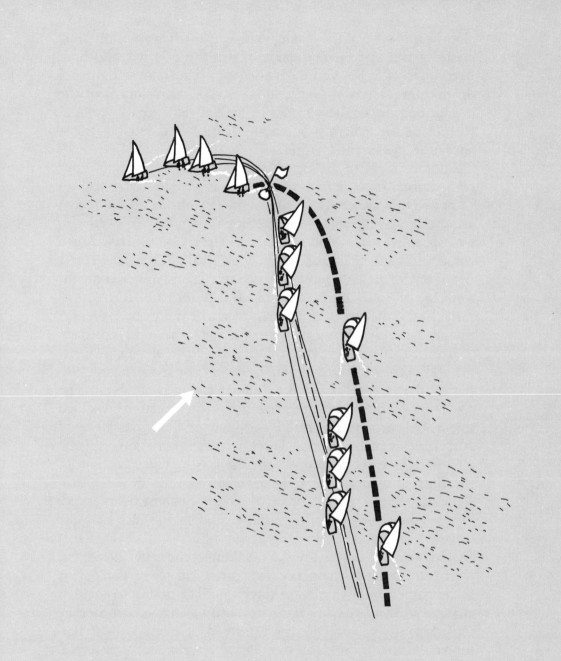

FIGURE 26

If you see that you are surely going to round fourth, bear off on the approach, so that you can take the mark close aboard starting the windward leg. Then you will not only have the freedom to tack if you so elect, but a good chance of riding over the two boats ahead of you, which are getting a big dose of backwind.

close in the wake of the inside boat. You are then apt soon to be ahead of the two boats outside of her and you will also have freedom to tack. See figure 26. You simply must not sit tight and do nothing. That's a pretty sure way to round fourth of the group. For any of these tactics to have any chance of working, you have to use them soon enough, and "soon enough" translates into proper anticipation.

Another form of anticipation is to know the traits of your competitors. If you know one of them is a "luffer" who hates to be passed to windward on a reach and will luff sharply to prevent it even though the rest of the fleet is gaining, then it is better to attempt to pass him to leeward. It is helpful also to know which competitors are bold and which scare easily. It's usually better not to try for an aggressive pin-end start against a bold competitor. One of you (and it could be you) is apt to be forced over early. But, if the guy next to you is meek, he is not apt to press at the end and you have a great chance to get the number-one start.

A rather obvious, yet vitally important, form of anticipation is the ability to predict wind shifts, not only at the start, but also during the race. This is what sailboat racing is all about. The sport would be far less interesting if wind direction remained steady. On certain days and for certain wind directions the wind is steadier than on others. There is always variation, and the ability to forecast and to position your boat to take advantage of the shifts can mean the difference between a win and a bad showing. Wind shifts can be predicted by watching boats ahead, by scanning smoke or flags ashore, and in the case of more experienced sailors, by looking at wind lines on the water. It is relatively easy to detect a puff by looking at the water ahead, but with practice and experience you often can tell if the puff is accompanied by a change in direction. The ability to forecast changes in wind velocity translates into having the appropriate replacement jib ready to hoist instead of being caught flat-footed, losing ground by carrying the wrong jib for several damaging minutes.

Next time you break a sheet or a guy in a strong wind, don't consider it bad luck. Instead, blame yourself for not anticipating the possibility and having the sheet or guy doubled up. It was a great satisfaction a few years back while racing on *Salty Goose* in the Channel Race in England to break our Kevlar spinnaker sheet. The satisfaction stemmed from the fact that we knew

Kevlar becomes fatigued where it passes through a block. We had a second sheet reeved and lost nothing when the Kevlar one failed.

You can doubtless think of other examples in which proper anticipation has helped, and its lack has cost you races. Proper anticipation in its myriad forms is the heart and soul of racing success, the most basic key separating winners from losers.

One thing you can be sure of is that you will lose a lot if you are outside a group of boats rounding a leeward mark in unison. Number 14296 is killing speed in hopes of a hole opening up. If it does, she will pass a number of boats. If it doesn't, she is in a tough spot because she can't claim room on the boats just off her leeward bow. PETER BARLOW

11

OBJECTIVE ANALYSIS

I still remember coming home after winning my first formal race more than fifty years ago. It was in a five-boat fleet of Herreshoff Bullseyes, and I felt pretty clever having won by nearly a quarter of a mile. My dad had been watching, and I expected him to shower me with praise. Although he did have a twinkle in his eye, his first words surprised me: "Nice work, but do you know why you won, and do you know what you did wrong?"

I had been in such a state of euphoria that I had not really given the race much thought. Dad's question set me thinking. The more I thought the more I realized I had won not through any great brilliance on my part, but through the mistakes made by my competitors. I realized also that our boat was going faster largely because it was the only boat that had a really clean bottom. I simply could not think of anything I had done wrong, especially on the last leg when I had increased my lead tenfold. "That's where you were wrong or lucky," Dad pointed out. "You had a lead, you were going faster, and you were wrong in going off on starboard tack when all the others went on port." "But that's where we did best," I complained. "Yes, I saw that," Dad countered, "but what if the wind had backed instead of hauling?

Since it did haul you won big; but if it had backed you would have lost. It would have been safer and better to have covered the others and won. Then you would have won by only one hundred yards instead of five hundred, but you would have been sure of winning. The course you took was the only way you could have lost. It didn't happen today, but on other days it will."

I felt a bit deflated, but I have thanked Dad ever since for instilling in me the habit of analyzing every race, by learning what I did right as well as what I did wrong—particularly what I did wrong.

Dad would never accept the explanation that I had been unlucky or that someone who beat me had been lucky. Sure, there is luck in yacht racing, but usually the luck (good or bad) is controllable and is the direct result of what you have done or failed to do. Blaming a loss on bad luck can stop you from putting your finger on the real reason.

There is one skipper in our local fleet who invariably sails high on a reach. He gains on the first two-thirds of the leg, and, unless the wind increases, he usually loses out approaching the mark. I have heard him complain many times how unlucky he was when the wind diminished and several boats went by despite the fact he had a big lead. He will never be a good sailor because he is not honest enough to blame himself for his mistakes.

Every race affords one an opportunity to learn, but it is an opportunity only for those who develop the habit of objective analysis. This applies to all levels of competition, but the very best sailors are the ones who continue to be critical and analytical, even after they have got to the top.

A smart skipper, provided he has a smart crew, will get the crew involved. When I was sailing for the America's Cup, especially in the close trial races, we made a habit of having an all-hands critique while sailing or being towed back to port. We had it whether we won or lost. Often, one of the crew members would come up with a mistake or a good move we had overlooked. We also had trained observers (in particular Olin Stephens) watching every minute of the race. After supper we would have a bull session. It became a game to see if we had already listed all the mistakes the observers had noted. Usually we had, but the mere fact that we knew these sessions were coming made us more alert, more aware of what we had done right and done wrong. Much more time was spent on our errors, even when we had won big.

Some skippers find it helpful to keep a diary of each race. In that way if they are honest in their appraisal of mistakes they might find a pattern of the same mistake recurring. That would give them a sure sign of what to improve on. Peter Scott kept the best diary I ever saw, complete with superbly rendered tactical diagrams. I've never kept a written diary of each race, but I do keep a mental one. I find it a big help to recollect what happened in a specific area or under specific conditions years before. When confronted by similar conditions in the same area, I then have a strong (albeit not certain) clue as to what will happen. But whether you keep a mental or a written diary (and you should do one or the other), the entries and observations have to be honest to be of real help. Excusing your mistakes will be counterproductive. On the other hand, sometimes a tactic or course that should have panned out doesn't. It is then vital to determine the reasons why it didn't work in this particular race. If you have sound reasons to believe the same course will work in the future, don't discard it simply because it didn't work once. And if you won big by a lucky or unusual wind shift, it is vital to recognize that it was unusual and not likely to be repeated in the future. If you do try it in the future and it doesn't work, don't blame it on bad luck. Instead blame yourself for not being sufficiently objective in your analysis of the first situation. Yacht racing wouldn't be the fascinating game it is if you could always predict what is going to happen. No one can. But objective analysis of each race will help immeasurably by improving your forecasting in races to come.

Buddy Melges, in preparing for the 1972 Olympics, had his sharp crew—Bill Allen and Bill Bentsen—write a critique of each series they entered for the entire year leading up to the Olympics. The critique covered not only tactics but also sail handling, sail trim, attitude, and ways boat speed might be improved. This not only reduced mistakes to an absolute minimum, but it also developed great team spirit. During a race there is often little time for conversation. In a large boat, except for the tactician or navigator, it is usually counterproductive and distracting to the skipper to have other crew members putting in their two cents' worth. Even so, if a crew member sees something important he feels the afterguard might have overlooked, he can and should *quietly* express his thoughts to the tactician. When I am skipper with a crew of, say, five or six, I welcome (except while concentrating on a start or in the midst of a ticklish maneuver) the thoughts of anyone aboard, assuming of course he is experienced. However, I want to hear the opinion *just once*. It is really distracting to have someone harping on his pet theory. Once a crew member is sure his suggestion has been heard, he should be quiet. There is a good chance the skipper was already weighing the pros and cons, and repetition of the same suggestion is not only distracting, but can also goad an uncertain skipper into making the wrong move.

Once the race is over, however, is the time for the most soul-searching analysis, the most critical comment from everyone on board. If you are the skipper, it is up to you to be the *most* objective, not only of the tactics and sail handling, but also of your own helmsmanship. If you know you have a good boat, fine sails, and an excellent crew, and yet your boat seems slower, then the fault may lie with the way you steer her. Once that thought has penetrated, you are on your way to doing something to improve your touch. You might decide to let someone else steer more, while you, as skipper, concentrate on tactics and sail trim. Rod Stephens is a good helmsman, but he spends little time at the wheel. He is objective enough to realize that his boat will do better if he concentrates on getting her trimmed to perfection and going the right way, two areas where he is not just good but superb. The fact that he steers less often than many others on board makes him no less a skipper. Quite the contrary. He has discovered the best possible way to win. Mike Vanderbilt is another such example. He recognized his shortcomings as an upwind helmsman in light air and let someone else (usually Sherman Hoyt) steer his J Boats upwind in such conditions. No one, though, ever doubted who was the skipper of *Enterprise, Rainbow,* and *Ranger.* It was Mike Vanderbilt— the epitome of the analytical man who never lets ego or vanity get in the way of winning.

Objectivity and analysis are important not just for a race but for a campaign. Lack of it on the part of challengers for the America's Cup is one reason why the Americans have always won. On many occasions the American defenders have been technologically superior, with better boats, better sails, and better equipment. In some of those years the challenger, though well sailed, had no chance at all. In recent years there has been little to choose between the boats, but invariably the Americans have sailed better. This was surely true as far back as 1934, and also in 1970 and 1980, when we could have lost had we not outsailed the challenger. Although Americans are second to none as sailors, we have no lock on brilliance. We just get our best sailors to defend, while the challengers all too often select good but not brilliant sailors who come from the "right" club.

When we lose the Cup, it will be to the determined head of a challenge syndicate who selects a world-class skipper from his country, not merely a good sailor he happens to know or one who comes from the right club.

Whether you are in a race at your own club or in a big yachting event, you will surely do better if you analyze why you won or lost with all the objectivity you can muster.

12

KNOW THE
RULES

*T*he subject of this chapter may seem almost too obvious to be called a key to success in yacht racing. If you are a neophyte, I am sure you would study the right-of-way rules before entering races without any prodding on my part. If you are an old hand, you are apt to conclude that you know the rules and that anything I might tell you in this chapter is superfluous. I contend, however, that unless you are extraordinary you do not know them well enough, and until you do you won't achieve your full potential as a racing skipper.

It is vital to know the rules instinctively so that in a tight situation you will not be intimidated, will not have to delay, and can focus your thoughts on the tactics of winning. If your mind is preoccupied with wondering whether or not you have right-of-way, you cannot think ahead. Worse still, you just might be disqualified.

This chapter is not designed to teach you the rules except in a cursory way. It would take an entire book to make you a rules expert. My purpose here is to convince you, if I can, how vital it is to know them cold and to demonstrate how to go about it.

A few examples might prove the point. When I was a teen-ager, I was privileged to race on Long Island Sound in the

International One Design Class, as competitive a group as you will ever find. In my very first start I was well positioned, just fetching the windward end of the line. I was startled to hear one of the great sailors of the class, who was overlapped on my weather quarter, shouting at me for room to cross. Fortunately for me he had picked a rule I happened to know well. In those days you did have to give room after the starting signal (you don't now), but not before the gun fired. We were at the stern of the committee boat before the gun. Without any hesitation I shouted at my august competitor, "I'm going to drive you right through the committee boat." He didn't say a word, but he luffed up fast. This not only got me a good start (and forced one of my toughest competitors into a bad one), but it also earned me a reputation (not then fully deserved) for knowing the rules cold. As a result, none of my more experienced peers ever again tried to intimidate me or press me too much. It may not be proper to ask for rights that you don't have (and in fact I deplore the practice), but you'd better believe it is done quite frequently.

It is not just club sailors who sometimes foul out of a race because of ignorance of a rule. The America's Cup match is as important a race as there is, and you might expect those who compete for it to be really up on the rules. Most are, but Jim Hardy, skipper of *Gretel II* in the 1970 match, was not. He lost a race at the protest table after he had won it on the race course. It may have cost him the America's Cup. He did win another race, and except in very heavy air he had the faster boat.

At the start, *Intrepid* was barging on *Gretel's* weather quarter. Prior to the gun, *Gretel* kept squeezing up (as was her right) to close the gap between her and the committee boat. *Intrepid* was in a vulnerable spot because, if the gap was closed, she had no right to ask for room. But when the starting signal was hoisted and the gun fired, there was still just enough room for *Intrepid* to pass between *Gretel* and the committee boat, provided *Gretel* then assumed a close-hauled course as the rules require. Bill Ficker, skipper of *Intrepid,* drove for the line. To his surprise, instead of bearing off, *Gretel* kept luffing above close-hauled, and a collision occurred. Hardy quite obviously knew the basic part of the rule, which states: "When approaching the starting line to start, a leeward yacht shall be under no obligation to give any windward yacht room to pass to leeward of a starting mark surrounded by navigable water." He also knew that when approaching the line he could luff up to head to wind to make sure there was no room. But just as obviously, he was not familiar with the next part of the pertinent rule, 42.4, which follows that quoted above. It reads: " . . . but, after the starting signal, a *leeward yacht* shall not deprive a *windward yacht* of room at such a *mark* by sailing either above the compass bearing of the course to the first *mark* [which he had not], or above *close-hauled* [which he had].

How am I so sure that Hardy was ignorant of this rule? I'm sure because I was one of the very first to talk to him after the race. After congratulating him on sailing a fine race, I commiserated with him about the foul. When he seemed completely unworried, I asked him if he had luffed above close-hauled after the starting signal. "Sure," he said. To be certain, I repeated the question, asking if he had done so after the gun had fired. "Yes, we were trying to squeeze *Intrepid* out," was the reply. I am sure Hardy must at one time have known this limitation on the leeward boat's rights, but in the heat of battle he forgot it. One of the greatest victories in his life was snatched away from him at the protest table the next day.

How do you learn the rules so well that this does not happen to you? I think an effective way is first to learn the basic rules, then the exceptions, when the basic rules are modified.

The United States Yacht Racing Union has printed what they term the *Yacht Racing Right-of-Way Rules in Brief.* They emphasize that they are simplified, condensed, and unofficial, intended only as an aid to newcomers to the sport, not as a substitute for the official rules. However, if you know them, you can keep out of trouble and at the same time stand up for your rights about 95 percent of the time. With that thought in mind, and with the thought of using them as a stepping-stone to a complete understanding of the rules, these simplified rules are printed here:

1. *Port-starboard.* When yachts are on opposite tacks (booms are on different sides), port tack (yacht with boom on starboard side) keeps clear (see Rule 36).
2. *Windward-leeward.* When yachts are on the same tack (booms on the same sides), the windward yacht keeps clear, or the yacht astern keeps clear (see Rule 37).
3. *Changing tack.* When you are tacking or jibing, keep clear of other yachts. After you tack or jibe and you suddenly get right-of-way, give the other yacht room and time to keep clear (see Rule 41).

4. *Luffing before starting.* Before you start, you may luff a yacht to windward, but you must do it slowly (see Rule 40).

5. *Barging.* At the start, don't "barge." That means don't try to squeeze between a yacht close to leeward of you and a starting-line mark, which probably is a race-committee boat (see Rule 42.4).

6. *Over early.* If you are over the line early at the start, keep clear of all yachts that have started properly as you return to restart (see Rule 44).

7. *Buoy room.* When you are two boat lengths from a turning mark, an obstruction, or a finish-line mark (which may be a race-committee boat), give room to all yachts that have an inside overlap on you (see Rule 42).

8. *Luffing after starting.* When another boat tries to pass you to windward, you may luff her until her skipper hails "mast abeam" (meaning her skipper is even with or ahead of your mast). Then you must stop luffing and bear off to your proper course (see Rule 38).

9. *Touching a mark.* If you touch a mark, you may continue racing only after completely circling the mark. If you touch a starting-line mark, you must wait until after you have started to circle it. While thus circling a mark, keep clear of other yachts (see Rules 52 and 45).

10. *Rule infringements.* If you infringe a rule while racing (you are racing from your preparatory signal until you clear the finish line), you are obligated to retire promptly. Sometimes the sailing instructions permit an alternative penalty such as the "720 Rule" or a percentage scoring penalty (see Rule 33 and Appendix e). Even when you have right-of-way, it is your duty to avoid collisions (see Rule 32).

The danger in printing these simplified rules is that you may conclude they are all you need. Remember that Item 5, "Barging," is the basic rule that Jim Hardy knew, but there is no reference (except for the mention to see Rule 42.4) that warns the leeward yacht about her obligations and the limitations on her rights. Still, by starting with these basic simplified versions of the rules and then thinking about the modifications to them, you are well on your way to a complete knowledge.

Take the port-starboard rule. It implies that, if on starboard, you have full rights. Not so! If returning on a starboard tack from a premature start, you have to give way to port-tack yachts that have started correctly (see Rule 44). Also, when on starboard you must not so alter course as to prevent the other yacht from keeping clear. Another exception comes when you are on starboard tack approaching a leeward mark overlapped by an inside port-tack yacht. The port-tack yacht must be given room to round the mark (see Rule 42).

Actually, almost all of the exceptions and modifications to the simplified unofficial rules make good common sense. So, when in doubt, doing what seems logical will usually work out. But since "usually" is not sufficient, the rules in their entirety must be read with care, especially the right-of-way rules in Part IV of the official rules. Since they occupy a great many pages, they seem at first quite forbidding; but if you know the simplified rules, understanding the exceptions and the limitations to them will be easy.

This chapter is intended to advise you on how you might teach yourself the rules, and, it is hoped, to convince you of how important the whole exercise is. Toward that end, let's take a careful look at Rule 42—Rounding or Passing Marks and Obstructions. More protests are lodged under this one rule than all the others combined, so you should know it cold. Note at the outset that it is in Section C, and, as the preface states, "When a rule of this section applies, to the extent to which it explicitly provides rights and obligations, it overrides any conflicting rule in Section B, Principal Right-of-Way Rules and their Limitations, except Rule 35 (Limitations on Altering Course)."

Rule 42.1 is concerned with buoy room, Item 7 of my simplified code. Note, however, how many modifications apply.

1. Rule 42.1 doesn't apply to a starting mark surrounded by navigable water.
2. It does apply to an obstruction.
3. The room to which the *inside* yacht is entitled does extend to giving her room to tack and jibe [42.1(a)].
4. The inside yacht, after getting this room, must jibe to assume the direct course to the next mark [42.1(b)].
5. But she need not if she has luffing rights [42.1(b)].
6. On a beat an inside port-tack yacht does not have rights for room over a starboard-tack yacht [42.1(c)].

*More protests occur rounding leeward marks than in any other situation.
The leaders rounding abreast are all observing the rules, but the ones on
the outside will lose a number of places. Number 1221 can't claim room on
them, but she has a fine chance of following 1218, taking room that was
there and passing a number of boats. But if she forces an overlap she is out.*

7. You don't have to give room at a mark if you have luffing rights and you also pass the wrong side of the mark [42.1(d)].
8. But to be legal in the above (Item 7), the leeward yacht must hail to that effect and begin to luff before the two-length circle [42.1(d)].

Let me interrupt at this point to illustrate how familiarity with my eighth point, above, is important not only to keep from being disqualified, but also to make the maneuver effective. When I was skipper of the Twelve Meter *Courageous* in the 1974 final trial races against *Intrepid,* we were being overtaken on the second reaching leg. *Intrepid* gained an overlap at about fifteen lengths from the mark, and we guessed she would be abeam of us by the time we reached the mark. We therefore decided to take her to windward of the mark and headed for a spot about one length to weather of it. About five or six lengths from the mark, *Intrepid* hailed for room. If we had informed her at that point that we were taking her to weather of the mark, she would have been sufficiently forewarned perhaps to negate the effectiveness of the maneuver. Therefore, we said nothing. Instead both Ted Hood, my tactician, and I looked under the boom at the mark. I had planned to wait until two and a half lengths from the mark, and Ted, who knows the rules cold, must have had the same notion, because when we were just under three lengths, as I was about to hail our intentions to *Intrepid,* Ted hailed them. He stated that we were taking them the wrong side of the buoy. By waiting until the last moment, we caught *Intrepid* napping. After passing the mark, we were able to jibe to go back while she had to tack to return. As a result we rounded two lengths ahead. If we had not hailed prior to the two-lengths circle, we would have been disqualified. If we had hailed sooner than we did, we wouldn't have got such a big advantage.

Now let's go back to an analysis of the exceptions in Rule 42 to Items 5 and 7 in the simplified rules.

9. Note that, when jibing is an integral part of the rounding maneuver, a yacht clear ahead may jibe to round the mark or obstruction without having to worry about jibing too close [42.2(a)]. This is an exception to Rule 31.1.
10. Note also that she may not tack to round if she cannot keep clear while so doing. In this instance Rule 41.1 remains in force.

11. Even though the simplified rule says you must gain an overlap prior to the two-length circle, there can be an instance when you have gained it prior to that, say three or more lengths, and would still be disqualified if sufficient room were not given to miss both the mark and the outside yacht. Such an instance could be in a hard breeze with both boats planing for the mark. If you gain an overlap at three or four lengths from the mark, the outside yacht must then attempt to give you room to round wide. If, because of the speed of approach, or because the leading yacht is having control problems, it *cannot* give the required room, the inside yacht is disqualified even if she gained an overlap four lengths from the mark [42.3(i)].

12. The above is true because the yacht clear ahead has no obligation to give room before an overlap is established. In short, she need not anticipate the fact that she may be unable to give room in time [42.3(b)]. The onus of proving when the overlap was established is on the inside yacht [42.3(d)].

13. Even if an overlap is broken after reaching the two-length circle, the inside yacht must still be given room [42.3(c)]. If an outside yacht claims the overlap was broken prior to reaching the two-length circle, the onus is then switched to her to prove that she did indeed break it at a greater distance [42.3(e)].

14. There is a situation in which an "overlap" can be established inside the two-length circle and room can be claimed. When you read the definition of overlap you will find it applies only to yachts on the same tack, *except* when Rule 42, Rounding Marks and Obstructions, applies. There, the boats can be considered overlapped even though on opposite tacks. Rule 42.3(a)(ii) specifically provides that, if two yachts are approaching a mark on a beat on opposite tacks, one can tack to leeward of the other yacht inside the two-length circle and still be entitled to ask for room to round the mark. If it is then too late for the yacht on a tack to luff up and give the room, the tacking yacht is out. The yacht on the tack must, however, so luff as soon as the other has completed her tack. In practice, there is usually sufficient opportunity to provide room even if a yacht tacks to leeward of

another that is just one length from the mark, since luffs can be executed swiftly.

15. A clear astern yacht cannot claim room to clear a continuing obstruction unless there was room between the obstruction and the leading yacht prior to establishment of the overlap. In short, she cannot ask the leading yacht to widen out to provide room [Rule 42.3(f)].

16. One of the exceptions to Item 5, "Barging," in the simplified code, has already been discussed in relation to the *Gretel II–Intrepid* protest, when Hardy forgot his obligation to bear off to a close-hauled course at the starting signal.

The other exception to Item 5 is the obligation of the leeward yacht to assume a course no higher than the compass *bearing* of the course to the first mark. This limitation is more complicated than it might appear. After clearing the starting line, the proper course of a leeward yacht could very easily be as much as twenty degrees above the compass bearing of the first mark. If a strong current were setting her to leeward, it could be. Moreover, if there were an obvious streak of heavy air up to windward, she could justify a high course on that basis. After clearing the line, such a course could be the proper course that she could assume after losing luffing rights, even though it was well above the direct compass heading for the mark. But until the starting line has been cleared, the leeward yacht must not sail above the compass bearing to the mark even if current might be creating such leeway that she could not possibly fetch the mark on that heading.

Do you think this is splitting hairs? An American yacht was disqualified on this very point in the Admiral's Cup race several years ago. Like all the exceptions, this rule does make sense because it clearly specifies the obligations of the leeward yacht and precisely determines the amount of room the windward yacht can expect at a critical moment of the race. But some of the sharpest racing skippers fail to realize the full import of that simple phrase "compass bearing of the course to the first mark."

You will be relieved to know that those are all the exceptions I can think of to Items 5 and 7 in the simplified code. Perhaps they have convinced you that the rules are a bit more complex than you realized. Rule 42 is by far the most complex. However, with a bit of study and thought, all these exceptions can be learned.

I do not believe in trying to memorize rules, and, in fact, there are many rules whose numbers I don't know. But I do care about knowing what my rights and my obligations are, and I have found that by learning the basic rule first and then thinking of the exceptions you will eventually get it down.

Note that I said "thinking of" the exceptions and modifications of the basic simplified code. I've listed sixteen of them applying to just one rule, 42.1, and if you asked me to list all sixteen from memory, I would be hard pressed to come up with more than half. Still, from thinking about the exceptions, when I get on the race course in a situation that applies, I quite instinctively do the right thing. If I, who not only don't have a photographic memory but in fact not a great memory at all, can do it, so can you. The exceptions all make good common sense; so if you study the rules with some care and ferret out the fine points that were not familiar, you are pretty sure of doing the right thing in regard to the rules when you get on the race course. If you think you are right but are not positive, then be sure to avoid a collision. If you think you might be the burdened vessel, you probably are, and you had better give way. Eventually, if you race enough, you will encounter enough situations to gain an instinctive knowledge of right-of-way in any incident. For example, instead of trying to memorize the wording of the rule that requires a boat after the starting signal to bear off to a close-hauled course, or on a reaching start to a compass heading no higher than the first mark, think instead of the *Gretel II-Intrepid* protest. You will never forget the pertinent rule.

Another effective way to learn the rules is to look at boats in close proximity and ask yourself which one(s) have right-of-way. Come up with snap answers. There is simply no time during a race to think why. Then, after having given the snap answer, take time to analyze why you answered as you did and determine what specific rule or rules governed the case. You will be pleased to see that most of the time you will be correct. When not correct this mental exercise is a great way to insure that you will be right the next time. Only when you are always correct in your snap judgment can you tell yourself that you know the rules well enough to maneuver with daring in a tight situation. Only then can you say you know the racing rules.

Before closing our discussion of rules, there is one other caveat worth mentioning. Be sure you know which yacht has the burden of proof in various situations. For example, a yacht establishing an overlap at a mark has the burden of proving she established it soon enough. If the protest committee is in doubt, the inside yacht will be thrown out for having gained it too late. If the overlap is broken just near the two-length circle, the outside yacht has the burden of proving it was broken outside of two lengths rather than inside.

In a crossing situation, if the starboard-tack yacht says a collision would have occurred if she had not borne off, the port-tack yacht has to prove that such was not the case. In the absence of witnesses, that's almost impossible. The same applies to tacking or jibing closely. You have to prove you didn't do it too closely.

Whenever the burden of proof is on you, that's the time not to press and to be *sure* you have not violated a rule. It is particularly dangerous to cross closely in front of an inexperienced sailor who is on starboard tack. Not being too adept at gauging distance, he is apt to bear off unnecessarily to avoid a collision that he thought was imminent. If he then protests, you are on thin ice indeed, even if you know you were right and could have crossed. It is far safer to do it when racing against an expert. If you are going to cross closely in front of a boat, one precaution is to hail him to hold his course. You had better be right, however. I once did that in full expectation of clearing his bow, only to have him tick my transom. That was not only embarrassing, but it also put me out of the race.

Let me point out, in closing, that although knowledge of the rules will enable you to maneuver in close quarters and in fast-changing situations with confidence, it is important to avoid protest situations. The best sailors can misjudge, even if they know the rules. Moreover, we all have seen instances when an inexperienced protest committee threw out the wrong boat. Therefore, once you have the rules down cold, play it bold, but not too bold. It is not wise to initiate a protest in a questionable situation, even though you know you cannot be thrown out because the burden of proof is on the other skipper. He will remember that. In another race the circumstances might be reversed, and he just might protest you in a situation when it is up to you to prove your innocence.

The rules are designed to prevent collisions and to prevent one yacht from being unfairly disadvantaged. They are not designed to encourage protests. In flagrant violations, and even in somewhat minor but definite violations, a protest is warranted. There are, after all, no umpires on the race course. Do not, however, develop into a sea lawyer, intent on seeking ways to disqualify your opponents. Not only can this backfire if you develop such a reputation, it also makes yacht racing less fun, which, when all is said and done, is why we are out there.

13

READ THE CIRCULAR AND SIGNALS

I entered the final race of the Raven Class Nationals in 1951 three points out of first, and I was determined to go all out to put the necessary two boats between me and the current leader. Since we had beaten each other the same number of times in the preceding four races, a tie would be decided in my favor. I went for the number-one start at the favored end of the line and managed to take it. The course was windward-leeward-windward, to Mark A near the shore, a run to Mark O, and then a beat home.

After a good start I played the shifts in the puffy northwester so effectively that I had a fifty-yard lead at the first mark. Until this race, I had done only so-so upwind, but with a light crew had excelled downwind. So things were looking good, especially since the series leader was buried in sixteenth place at the first mark. I expected he would work his way up, but if I held onto first he would have to climb to third to win the series.

I jibed on the lifts, planed away from the competition, and rounded Mark O a hundred yards ahead of the second boat. As I sheeted in for the beat home, I could see that the series leader had picked up a few boats, but his cause looked hopeless.

The second boat to round split tacks with me, but the third, fourth, and fifth boats were following my upwind course. I could now see that the boat I had to beat would be the twelfth to round. With just a two-and-a-half-mile beat to go in a fresh wind, it seemed there was no way I could lose. The fact that there were the big wind shifts typical of a northwester didn't perturb me. It would give my rival a chance to pass a number of boats if he picked everything right; but third place seemed impossible.

I was feeling on top of the world. Then I looked back to check on the boats astern and was puzzled to see the sixth boat sail past the mark and continue on to leeward with spinnaker set. The puzzlement turned to alarm when the seventh boat followed her! "Get me the circular," I shouted, and at the same time eased off the sheets, already sensing the worst. Sure enough, there was a Mark Q a mile farther to leeward of Mark O. "Are you sure the second mark was O and not Q?" I asked my crew. "We read it as O, but we're not sure," they replied. I had read it as O also, but suddenly it dawned on me that we had all failed to see that little squiggly tail that turns an O into a Q. There is no way the sixth and seventh boats would have continued downwind unless they had been sure that the leeward mark was Q, not O.

We had never set a spinnaker so fast, despite its not being ready, and soon thereafter the four boats that had been following us upwind set theirs, as the bitter truth dawned on them too. We rounded Mark Q in eleventh place, two lengths ahead of the series leader, who was twelfth. We still had a chance to pull it off if we could put two boats between us. Instead of covering him we tacked in the headers, but he was too smart and kept following us. We started picking up boats, but he did also. Finally, a hundred yards from the finish, we moved into seventh place with the leader now ninth. There was one boat just ahead of us, but we were clear of her backwind and gaining. If we could catch her, we would still win. We were gaining so fast it was just a question of whether the race would last long enough. When we hit the line, two lengths to windward on his quarter, there was no way of telling whether we were sixth or seventh, and the whole series hung in the balance. The whistles were as nearly simultaneous as is possible. We tacked over to the committee boat and asked if we were sixth or seventh.

"A dead heat for sixth," was the reply. It took us a second or two to digest the fact that by tying for sixth we had lost the series by half a point, instead of being tied for the lead on points and winning by virtue of a tie-breaking formula.

It was a bitter pill to swallow, but we could blame only ourselves. The fact that the host yacht club thereafter abandoned letter Q on their signals as being too hard to differentiate from O was no excuse. Others had read it correctly, and we had been careless in not putting binoculars on the signal to be sure. The fact that still other boats read it incorrectly also did us in. If we had been the only boat to head upwind after passing Mark O, we would have learned of our mistake soon enough to keep the necessary two boats between us and the series winner. We were not the only careless ones, but that doesn't change the fact that we *were* careless and deserved what we got. If I had studied the circular ahead of time, I might have noted that, looking from Mark A, Marks O and Q were directly in line, and I might have taken more care to be sure that I was not mistaking one signal for the other.

Is this an extreme and isolated example of the perils of not reading the circular or course signals with sufficient care? Extreme, yes, but by no means isolated. A great many of the finest sailors in the world have lost races by failing to read or to digest a circular.

In an Admiral's Cup race in the Solent a few years ago, a boat on the American team was disqualified for passing inside a limit mark. The race instructions were extremely long. On page 16 they specified that, when going downward past the starting line, you must not only not cross the starting line, but you must also go outside of a small round buoy set outside the line. The intent is to keep the starting and finishing area clear at all times for the great number of classes that assemble at Cowes. I know how the Admiral's Cup participant felt because the very next day I did the same foolish thing in my boat, not then realizing why she had been disqualified. I was even more foolish because as I approached that insignificant-looking buoy, I asked our navigator if it was anything we had to observe. "Nothing in the circular," he replied. He was correct that it wasn't shown on the chart, but it *was* referred to in the fine print on page 16! We had both read the circular, but obviously not with sufficient care. We cut the buoy by half a boat length, gaining nothing in the process. The boat astern waited till we were a quarter mile past to inform us of our error. By then a race we had been winning turned into our worst finish of the week.

A few years ago a boat that would have won the Bermuda Race was deprived of victory by cutting Kitchen Shoal buoy five miles from the finish of the 637-mile course. She had not meant to. The skipper had failed to read the circular with sufficient care to note that this buoy was a mark of the course. The two-hour penalty that was assessed dropped him from first in the fleet to a mediocre finish. A couple of years before, I saw another foreign boat do the same thing. She rated the same as we did at the bottom of Class F and was about half a mile behind us. I hated to protest them because they had sailed a good race, gained little by cutting the buoy, and would have placed third in their class if they had rounded the mark. Still, a rule is a rule. I called it to their attention, and they informed the race committee of their error.

We also had a bit of a disappointment in that race since we missed winning our class by just two minutes. Fifty miles from the finish we identified the boat that eventually cut Kitchen Shoal buoy and determined from the scratch sheet that she had the same rating as we did. Since we had a feeling we were doing well in our class, and since we were then one hundred yards ahead of the rival we had sighted, it seemed important to be sure of beating her across the line. Hence, we match-raced her and in the process lost an estimated five minutes from what we would have recorded by sailing our own course to the finish. If the situation were to happen again, I think I would do the same thing again because it seemed of paramount importance to beat her across. Perhaps I'm wrong, because in a class numbering thirty-seven boats we had many unseen rivals to consider. At least we hadn't misread the circular.

The examples I have cited were all in highly competitive fleets, and are but a few of the many in which misreading the circular or signals has affected the outcome of a race. If you have raced a great deal, I'm confident you can recall instances when it has done you in, or done in boats you were racing against.

It is important to read carefully not only circulars and sailing instructions, but also any other data affecting the race. For example, Eldridge lists the time the current changes direction in Long Island Sound, Block Island Sound, Martha's Vineyard, Buzzard's Bay, and Nantucket. I have referred to it for so many years that it is one publication I know almost as well as the back of my hand. Perhaps it was because of this familiarity that I

This picture brings back sad memories. It shows us in Witch *crossing the finish of the 1972 Bermuda Race to take second in class. That part isn't sad, but the code flag "B" in our rigging is. We are protesting a boat that cut inside of the Kitchen Shoal buoy five miles from the finish. Had they not cut it, they would have placed third in a class of over thirty boats. They failed to read the circular specifying Kitchen Shoal as a mark of the course and hence after 637 miles of keen sailing had two hours added to their time. I seldom protest, but when a boat fails to sail the prescribed course I feel compelled to, even though it hurts.*

looked at it too hastily a couple of years ago when racing at Block Island Week. I referred to the wrong column and noted the time the current was to turn east as the time it actually turned west. I couldn't imagine why the bulk of the fleet was taking a course that would be suicidal in an easterly current and was preening myself on being one of the few smart ones there. Imagine my chagrin when I saw them getting kicked to the west by the current after clearing the southwest point of the island instead of being sucked to leeward in an easterly direction as my quick reading of the tables would have indicated. Upon seeing this, I rechecked Eldridge, and found in an instant how careless I had been. By then it was too late to recoup.

It is advisable to get the circular and sailing instructions several days in advance. Read them in the quiet of your home, not on the way out to the start when other things will be grabbing your attention. Underline or note any special features. Do not assume that, since most sailing instructions are comparable, the ones for the race in question will be standard. Make special note of any government marks that must be observed.

Note whether the around-the-ends rule applies after a general recall (or even on the first start, which is occasionally the case). Note also when the next start is to take place after a general recall. The time can vary, and knowing the right interval is imperative. Many boats won't be sure; they will either start incorrectly or waste valuable time checking instead of concentrating on getting a good start.

The interval between the preparatory and warning signal is almost always five minutes, but on rare occasions it is three. I remember once when it was three minutes, and a number of boats were more than four minutes from the line when the three-minute preparatory signal was made!

After reading the circular and instructions it is a good idea to circle the pertinent marks on the chart. Also make a note as to whether or not the finish mark has to be observed on a twice-around windward-leeward course in which the start and finish are midway between the windward and leeward marks. Sometimes it is illegal to cross such a line when on the long windward leg; at others it is perfectly legal. The sailing instructions will tell you.

As soon as course signals are hoisted, have *at least two* people read them independently. Then, *write down the mark letters* and their sequence. It is vital to write them down. If a boat ahead of you rounds the wrong mark, it is all too easy to fall into the trap of believing she must be right. If you have it written down, you will be sure, and you will have the courage not to repeat her mistake. Remember the perils of being a sheep.

After the signals have been checked and the marks written down, have at least one person check the signals immediately after the warning signal. Changes can be, and often are, made at the warning signal or shortly before it. Failure to recheck can be disastrous.

A classic example of the damage that can come from failing to read the circular is the rare case when the finish of a day race is in a different location from that of the start. In most day races one finishes at the position of the start. Whenever the finish is moved, the sailing instructions so specify! But sailors are so used to finishing where they started that, unless they read the circular, at least a few will automatically head back for it. The Danmark Trophy race run by the Stamford Yacht Club is a case in point. The course signals merely specify the turning marks, and unless you have read the instructions after rounding the last mark, you are apt to head back to the starting area to finish. For that particular race the club elects to finish at the entrance to Stamford Harbor to lure boats into staying around for the awards party immediately after the race. Despite clear instructions, every year a few foolish yachtsmen head for the starting area after rounding the last turning mark. How do I know they do this? Partly because I have observed them doing it, and partly because one year I was one of those damn fools. In the process I lost a position or two until I realized that I was one of the few boats heading in that direction. I rechecked the circular and corrected my error before many competitors realized how dumb I had been.

Since so many races are lost and so many positions sacrificed through failure to read the race circular and instructions with proper care, reading, studying, and remembering them must be included as one of the real keys to racing success. Doing so will not in itself guarantee success, but it is certainly a key way to avoid failure.

14

COMPETE AGAINST THE BEST

*T*here is a truism in sailing, just as in many other sports, that you will progress little beyond the level of competition to which you are exposed. It is impossible, for example, to become a good tennis player if you compete only against people who poop the ball back. Playing against someone better than you will surely improve your game.

A runner simply cannot post the times he is capable of unless he enters meets with runners faster than he is. At first he may lose, but he will almost surely run faster than he ever has before. If he then has enough natural talent, he just might start winning against the hotshots. There is nothing quite like chasing someone really good to bring out the best that is in you and thereby do better than you thought you possibly could.

Sometimes you don't even have to have a physical opponent to improve as a runner; a standard to aim at may be enough. For example, until Roger Bannister broke the four-minute barrier for running the mile in 1954, all of the world's great milers concluded that that was just too fast for a human being to cover the distance. Once Bannister had proved it was possible, a veritable host of runners ran under four minutes. The record now stands at under 3:48 and counting, which means that the four-minute miler, who not too long ago was considered the ultimate achiever, would now be something like 90 yards behind today's best.

In sailing, competing against top-flight sailors not only stimulates you to improve your boat speed and your tactics, but it also provides a superb learning opportunity if you take time to analyze how the winners achieve victory. If you open your eyes, you will see how their boats are rigged, tuned, and equipped to go faster than yours. You can observe how they go about getting good starts. You can learn from their tactics and from how they seem to be able to smell out wind shifts so as to be in the right place at the right time. You can watch how they gain ground at turning marks, instead of being buried as you so often are. After a while, you might, if you are intrinsically good, start winning. Once you do win with regularity, it is time to seek out still better competition if you hope to become really good. If you don't, you will stagnate.

You might even conclude that you are such hot stuff that you know it all; but the really good sailors don't feel this way. They realize that there is always more to learn. With that realization, they have a chance of staying on top against the very best. Without such awareness it is only a matter of time before someone who has kept learning knocks them off. But if that happens to a top sailor, he then has a chance to improve his own ability, once again becoming number one, providing he keeps competing against the best. Resting on your laurels and avoiding the sternest tests is a sure way to become number two and eventually numbers three and four.

It is time for a few examples. When I was a youngster, I started to win with regularity in the Herreshoff Bullseye Class. I liked winning and even concluded I was a hot sailor. My dad knew better. He realized that if I was ever to be any good it was time to move on. Hence, he bought an Atlantic Class sloop for me to race. When I began finishing in the middle of the fleet, I realized I wasn't so hot after all. Three years later I won the fleet championship, but instead of letting me savor likely wins in the years ahead, Dad moved me into the International One Design Class. There, for the first time, I was up against *really* good sailors, and it was from them that I learned enough skills to hold my own in a variety of competitive classes down through the years.

I have never been a good dinghy sailor, being somewhat lacking in coordination, but for years I competed in the frostbite fleet at Larchmont Yacht Club. The best I ever did for the season was third, but because of the experience I gained there, I have managed to do well in other dinghy fleets, despite not being a natural at this type of racing.

Why does the United States International Sailing Association spend so much of the money it raises to send our best young sailors abroad to sail in world championships? The answer is obvious. No one, however naturally talented he may be, can become a world-class sailor unless he is exposed to world-class competition.

Before Eric Heiden won all five speed-skating events in the 1980 Olympics, he had already competed abroad for several years. Only a handful of Americans go in for speed skating, so despite Eric's natural ability, he couldn't have driven himself to the top in the Olympics had he not gone to countries where skating was a major sport.

Our skiers have won only rarely in world competition, but by competing in World Cup events they are becoming steadily better. If they had stayed in the United States, having fun taking turns beating each other, they would not have been in the hunt at all when the last Olympics came around. Instead, they made a creditable showing.

There's a famous American yacht club whose members have done well in international competition for many years and have even won Olympic medals. I'll not mention its name because I know many of the members and don't want to insult them when I say that even their best sailors are not nearly as good as they might be. Their international competition has been limited to Eight Meters, Six Meters, and large, costly ocean racers. Sixes are as nice a boat to race as I know, but, being a development class, the design of the boat is as important as how she is sailed in determining who wins. Having better boats lulled some of these good sailors into believing they were great. At home, the members of this club usually raced only against one another, and even the best of them seldom branched out into more competitive classes. As a result, now that Meter boats are no longer being sailed locally, and now that ocean racing has become so much more competitive, you seldom see a winner from this club.

I'm not condemning what they did. They have had a ball competing against one another and competing abroad with superior tools; but because they have not been up against the best sailors, they have never achieved greatness.

Two members of this club had a go at America's Cup competition. Both of them failed. I suspect they failed not because they were poor sailors, but because they had never before been exposed to that level of competition. Neither one tried a second time. Had they done so, they just might have succeeded. They were knowledgeable sailors, but they lacked experience in top competition. The first time they were exposed to it they couldn't cut it.

Ted Turner is a perfect example of what I am driving at. Ted is a great sailor, but I do not feel he is a natural. It took him many years to win his local club championship, but as soon as he did he went farther afield, seeking new challenges. He switched from one designs to ocean racers, and thereafter mixed his sailing between the two. He competed for many years in the Congressional Cup with only mediocre results, but finally he won it—the first yachtsman not from the West Coast to do so. He failed miserably in his first America's Cup effort, largely because he had a poor boat. Next time out he won. But instead of resting on his laurels and protecting his reputation, he gave it a try a third time. He keeps going back to the Congressional Cup and is now one of the toughest of all to beat. He has been named Yachtsman of the Year four times, and as I write this he is still competing in the toughest of leagues, the very racing in which he and anyone else is sure to lose more often than win. By so doing, this sailor, who I still maintain is not a natural, remains a truly great one.

This does not mean that there is anything wrong with getting pleasure from racing on the club level. At my home yacht club the class that has the most fun and the greatest turnout is the least competitive. The better sailors in the club often look on with envy, but realize that if they joined that group they would probably win, but would get little satisfaction out of doing so. They prefer winning occasionally in a tougher league.

If you choose to sail in a low-level fleet, more power to you. But once you get a bit bored by winning too regularly, it is time to move on. It is surely time to move on if you hope to become a truly good sailor. You simply cannot become one by being dominant in a minor league or in a noncompetitive class.

It is helpful not only to compete against good sailors, but, if you can, to sail with them. In this way your knowledge is broadened more swiftly and more effectively than through any other method I know. I was blessed with a father who was a great sailor. Crewing for him when I was a youngster gave me an immediate advantage over other kids when I started sailing my own boat. In subsequent years I've crewed for such luminaries as Ted Hood, Briggs Cunningham, Bill Cox, Rod Stephens, Bob Derecktor, Ted Turner, and many other fine sailors. They all do things somewhat differently to achieve successful results, and the opportunity to learn has been enormous.

When Dennis Conner was young, he couldn't afford his own boat. He got crewing jobs with some of the hottest sailors around, and I'm sure this accelerated his learning process. Even if you are an established skipper, it is a great idea to crew on occasion with other good skippers. Crewing for a poor sailor is just too painful, even though it might teach you what *not* to do. Crewing for a good one is sure to be instructive, not only in tactics and helmsmanship, but also in sail selection and trim and the myriad little things that enable a hot sailor to get around the course faster. Don't limit yourself by always sailing your own boat!

The title of this chapter is perhaps a bit misleading. If you are not a fine sailor, it can be frustrating to race against the very best, even though you will improve in the process. What you should do if you hope to improve is sail against those who are at least a bit better than you are. Once you have reached their skill level, it is time to decide whether to enjoy that level of sailing or to establish still higher goals. Either way can be right. It all depends on what your approach to sailing is and what your goals are. Bear in mind, though, that to get better you must elect the hard way and accept sterner challenges.

15

BOAT SPEED

*T*here's nothing, absolutely nothing, that makes you appear smarter than a fast boat. Put another way, the canniest skipper in the world will look pretty stupid in a slow boat. Many people criticized Ted Turner when he was sailing *Mariner* in the 1974 America's Cup match. Eventually, he was relieved as skipper. Three years later, sailing *Courageous,* he received all sorts of kudos. I believe he did sail better in 1977, but the big difference was the relative speed of the two boats.

A whole book could be written on the various ways of developing the speed of your boat. Yet this will not be a long chapter, partly because we cannot cover each and every method, and also because I feel that the development of boat speed is not as complicated as many people make it out to be. Certain basics apply to all boats; we will focus on these.

We can quickly skip over the value of a smooth bottom since every racing skipper knows that this is important. Perhaps, however, you do not realize *how* important. After you think you have a really smooth bottom, go over it again with the finest wet and dry paper. It is impossible to get it too smooth. The bottom should have a flat finish, as opposed to a shiny one, since this best lets the water flow past. If you are really serious, the same applies to the topsides, part of which will be immersed. Glossy topsides look nice, but flat ones are faster. Never, never wax either your bottom or topsides.

The importance of good sails cannot be overemphasized. If you can convince your sailmaker to go out with you, by all means do so. The sail has not been built that cannot be improved by minor recutting. Once your racing sails have neared perfection, use them only for the most important races. I well remember winning the Long Island Sound Lightning Championship in 1962, largely because we had superior boat speed. Six weeks later we went to the Nationals and fared poorly. You could conclude that this was simply because we were sailing in a tougher league. That's partly true, but it doesn't explain why several boats that we beat on the Sound did very well in the Nationals and had superior boat speed. After returning home, we did poorly in our local fleet, a fleet we had excelled in earlier. Our sails, though they still looked pretty good, had lost their drive. When we got new ones, we started to do well again. There are just so many hours of top speed in any sail. Once you know they are fast, treat them with kid gloves. Fold them carefully, and use them only for the most important races. In the 1977 America's Cup trials, *Courageous* had good boat speed in June. By the time of the July trials, she had lost her edge. But a couple of new jibs, ordered for the final August trials and recut to near perfection, enabled her to regain the winning edge.

Tuning is also of vital importance, and methods vary with different boats. On masthead rigs, the lower shrouds should be relatively loose, but on fractional rigs they should be nearly as tight as the uppers. Avoid sideways bend, but tune so that you can induce a fore-and-aft curve to flatten your main as wind increases. Proper mast chocking is also essential for producing a fair fore-and-aft bend.

This is Ted Hood's Robin *crossing the finish as winner of the 1968 Bermuda Race. I was privileged to be her navigator. We had a great skipper and crew, a great boat, and sails so flawless that top boat speed was assured in all conditions. There's nothing like owning the company to insure top sails, but you don't have to. All you need is the ability to recognize good sails from bad, to trim and stretch them correctly, and if they are bad, to cajole the sailmaker into recutting.* BERMUDA NEWS BUREAU

How can you be sure your tuning is correct, your sails are right? There are two key ways. Look with care at how the fastest boats in your class are set up and then copy them. You don't have to be furtive. Most top skippers are willing to share their knowledge. If not, there is nothing wrong with looking.

Lightnings once raced with little rake to their masts. A few hot skippers tried considerable rake and went faster. Only the unobservant failed to follow suit.

Another effective way to increase boat speed is to brush with one of the top boats in your class. If you are also pretty good, the other skipper will be only too happy to oblige, since he knows that the benefit will be mutual. One boat should be set up in a way that her skipper feels is optimum, and she should then remain so without change. The other boat can then brush, changing rake, shroud tension, sheeting angles, and angle of heel until the best combination is discovered. If you are beating the yardstick boat, then, *and only then,* share with him the knowledge you have gained, have him readjust and try it again. In this way both boats will improve. If one boat continues to win, or even if they seem to develop equal boat speed, try switching sails. There is no better way to determine your sails' effectiveness. All of this takes time, but it is well worth while. It is for this reason that the Twelves often have trial horses. You can get your own trial horse by working with a friend in your fleet. Your friend will henceforth be harder to beat, but so will both of you when you race elsewhere.

In addition to tuning and sails, it is often how you trim and how you steer that develop boat speed. As for trimming, one boat should remain constant, and the other should experiment. The experimenting boat should vary the sheeting base of the jib, either by changes on the track or with a Barber hauler, widening the angle as wind increases. As the wind builds speed, mainsail shape should be altered through traveler and backstay adjustments until the fastest settings are ascertained. Experiment with jib-halyard tension and main-Cunningham tension as draft control measures.

As a basic rule, the harder the wind strength, the more tension you should apply on the Cunningham, the more you should increase backstay tension, and the harder you should haul on the jib halyard. Another basic technique is to ease the traveler farther to leeward as the wind increases. Often you will go fastest with a big luff in your main. Be sure to change only one

These Solings are both trimmed to perfection. The poles are cocked to permit the spinnaker to draw effectively with the jib up. It will be hard for the second boat to pass, but since boat speed should be equal, one slip on the leader's part and she would be run over.

thing at a time. And as you go along make notes as to where the fastest settings are.

If you have a one-design ocean racer (or a day racer that allows more than one jib), try jibs of various sizes to learn which is most effective in various wind velocities. Experiment with reefing the main, and don't minimize the importance of a flattening reef, often effective upwind in air as light as eight or nine knots. Eventually you will build up a store of knowledge about the most effective sail settings, sheeting angles, and mast bend amounts for a given wind and sea condition.

If, after all this experimentation and after swapping sails, one boat continues to win, then try swapping boats. This can be embarrassing if one skipper continues to have the edge in either boat. There is only one answer—he knows how to sail faster! Better to find this out in such a friendly exercise than on the race course. If you are the slow skipper, try to figure out what you are doing wrong. Are you pinching, or driving off? If you seem to be doing neither, then you have learned that you simply do not have as good a touch at the helm. Better to know it, however, than to blame it on the fact that your boat is slow. You now know what to work on.

Here are a few generalities about how a helmsman can improve. In general it is better to think in terms of sailing fast, as opposed to pointing. There is a perfect groove, of course, for which you should strive. The real master can retain speed and point at the same time. If you have trouble doing both, at least sail fast. The most important single instrument is a speedometer. Get up to the fastest speed you can while sailing upwind, then point higher and see how close you can go while still maintaining most of your speed. If by heading three degrees higher on the wind you lose half a knot in speed, that's obviously a poor tradeoff. But if the loss is infinitesimal, it is probably worth it. Learn also to watch seas and to keep from being stopped by them. Above all, think boat speed.

This is particularly true as the wind increases. If your boat will sail to windward at a speed of six knots in a fifteen-knot wind, it should sail at least that fast in a twenty-five-knot wind. All too frequently, speed will drop below five knots under such conditions. If it does, you probably have too big a headsail, or do not have a sufficiently deep reef. Also try easing the traveler down and widening the sheeting angle of the jib either on a track or by a Barber hauler. It is essential, however you do it, to keep your

Look at these two photos of the same Finn's mainsail. In the top, the cunningham is eased and the draft is aft. In the bottom, the cunningham has been tensioned and the draft has moved forward.

These Finns are sailing fast. Travelers are down, and this, plus good hiking, a bendy rig, and adequate twist, enables them to sail flat—a must when beating in a centerboard boat.

boat from heeling too much. Until the wind approaches gale proportions or the seas build unduly, there is no excuse for losing boat speed to windward as the wind increases. Loss in speed could be caused by not feathering enough, thus achieving too much angle of heel by driving off. Whatever the answer, either by shortening down, widening the sheeting angle, feathering, or a combination of all three, speed should be retained until the weather gets really rough. Let me once again emphasize the importance of a good speedometer, preferably digital. It will tell instantly the effect of a change in trim or tuning.

Speed downwind must be retained in a light air by heading up in the light spots, driving off in the puffs, and, when on a run, by tacking downwind. In fresh air, speed can be built by carrying a spinnaker when many are fearful of doing so. It is all too easy to

*You don't have to know it is Buddy Melges to recognize that this Star is
going fast. The crew is hiking to perfection (Buddy, too). The touch on the
tiller is light; the boat is on her feet and obviously in the groove. Note that
Buddy keeps her there by feel and by looking at the water and wind, not
by looking at the sails.*

Here's Melges again, going like a bat on a hard spinnaker reach. The crew is hiking well out and aft, and the sails are not overtrimmed. The jib is eased to reduce heel, but would be trimmed in a lull. In a heavier puff the vang would be eased to keep the boat on her lines without excessive heel. A crew like this makes boat speed seem easy.

PETER BARLOW

Don't believe the theory that little can be gained on a reach. In the 1981 Block Island Race Week, our J-30, Fox, rounded the weather mark second, closely pursued by a group of other boats. On the ensuing four-mile reach we closed on the leader and opened eight lengths on our pursuers. They must not have rigged outboard leads for their jib sheets. Note also our traveler way down and our modest angle of heel in a twenty-knot wind. In the puffs we carried a big luff in the main to keep Fox on her feet.

pound your way upwind in thirty knots, and then fear that there is no way you can handle the boat with a chute up on the ensuing run. But don't forget that once you get on the run, if you can build a speed of ten knots, there is only a twenty-knot apparent wind strength left to cope with. A good boat and good crew should be able to handle that. Try it if you hope to win.

Like almost everything else in competitive racing, the development and retention of boat speed is a question of experimentation and objective analysis, coupled with a bit of work. There's nothing more important, however, if you hope to win.

16

HAVE FUN

I began this book by espousing the somewhat depressing thought that preparation and practice are essential to success on the race course. In subsequent chapters I have called attention to more interesting ways of winning and improving one's perform-ance. Although I believe that all are important, it is a joy to conclude with a chapter on the most important key of all— having fun!

The importance of fun is twofold: one, to do better in the mathematical sense of improving your record, and two, for the pure pleasure of it. Without fun it is time either to give up the sport or to pursue a less intense aspect of it that will still be rewarding for you.

How do I know that having fun is so important? In the simplest terms, it is important because it allows you to be sufficiently relaxed to do your best. In more physical sports it is well known that to reach peak performance you have got to stay loose. Golfers hit their longest drives when they are most relaxed. Trying to knock the cover off the ball usually results in two things: an errant hook or slice, or less distance if by some miracle the shot does go straight. The golfer who is enjoying himself is sufficiently relaxed to get the timing and tempo that alone can produce a really long drive.

I was surprised to read that even in such a physical sport as speed skating enjoyment was essential to peak performance. When Eric Heiden was being interviewed after winning five Olympic gold medals for speed skating, he was asked how he had been able to dominate the best skaters from countries where speed skating was a major sport. His explanation was that he felt he enjoyed it more. True, Eric practiced ad infinitum. True, he is superbly endowed physically. But the same is true of those he conquered. The difference is that they had grim determination, whereas he, along with the supreme effort he put into it, managed to have fun. By having fun he was able to remain loose enough to get the optimum result from his natural ability. The pure joy of achievement was the key.

If enjoying what you are doing can help improve performance in a physical sport such as speed skating, imagine what it can do in sailboat racing, in which mental acuity is more important than physical prowess. It is difficult to think straight when you are not relaxed, but ever so easy when you are enjoying yourself. By being relaxed you will steer faster and execute maneuvers and sail changes more efficiently. Why? Simply because you no longer have the impediment and distraction of stress. By having fun on the race course, however, I don't mean clowning around. It is important to have fun once the race has started, after having done all you can to prepare properly. Losing or doing badly in a sailboat race is not the end of the world. When you are doing badly, if you manage to keep from being upset, you then have a far better chance of improving. And even if you don't improve in that race, you will be in a better frame of mind to bounce back in the next one.

When he was still a youngster, Gene Walet entered the North American Sailing Championship for the Mallory Cup. He was sailing in strange boats (International One Designs), and had never before sailed on Long Island Sound. His chances looked dim. But he won one of the early races, and I can still remember the "rebel yell" from him and his crew as they rounded the first mark in the lead. They were having a ball, and their exuberance, instead of hurting their concentration, actually improved it. None of their opponents, many with big reputations, seemed to be having nearly as good a time. Gene went on to win the series in convincing style. Although he has done well since, I question if he has ever done so well in high-level competition as he did when he was too young to realize that sailboat racing is a serious sport. By this "failure" he sailed to the best of his formidable ability.

Paul Elvström has won more Olympic gold medals and more world championships than any other sailor. In one series he quit and went home, even though he was still in the running at the time. It was rumored that he had come close to a nervous breakdown. All of a sudden the burden of having to excel had become too much for him. A few years later a more relaxed Paul Elvström won still another world championship. Because sailing once again became fun, he had sailed up to his great potential.

My personal experience has taught me the importance of having fun to stay loose. When I was a senior in college, the Intercollegiate sailing championships were held in Class E scows. I had never sailed a scow before and didn't expect to do very well. Since we had won the year before in keel boats, we already had one title to our credit and didn't feel we had to prove ourselves. I looked forward to the series in scows as an opportunity to enjoy sailing a boat I had long been intrigued with, as opposed to a must-win situation. The first time we got onto a screaming plane I can well remember shouting with excitement and delight. Although we were not getting the most out of the scows, we were having so much fun that we were relaxed. Our starts, tactics, and sail handling were good. This enabled us to overcome our lack of familiarity with the boat, and I am sure this is why we won going away.

Many years later, when I became helmsman of *Constellation* in the 1964 America's Cup trials, the same thing happened. I was so excited about the prospect of sailing such a superb boat that I forgot to run scared. The pressure was eased further by the fact that when I did become helmsman in the later part of the summer we had never beaten our chief rival, *American Eagle*. As a result, we were not expected to win, and this reduced any mental strain I might have felt. If we could pull it off, that would be super; if not, no one would feel I was to blame. In the meantime how could anyone really "lose" when sailing such a beautiful racing machine?

With this relaxed but hardly carefree approach, I believe I sailed better than I ever have before or since. I was aided, of course, by the fact that *Constellation* was a fine Twelve. But since I was having fun, I was able to sail to the best of my ability, and this turned out to be enough to bring her home. It became even more fun as we kept winning; but even if we hadn't won, hadn't gained selection, and hadn't gone on to defend the cup, we would have enjoyed ourselves, secure in the knowledge we were sailing that lovely boat well.

Ten years later it was quite a different story. I was then skipper of *Courageous,* and we were favored to win. In early races against *Valiant* and *Mariner,* we won with such ease that our favorite's role was confirmed, and we entered the June trials full of confidence. There we met *Intrepid* for the first time, and it was a rude awakening. *Intrepid* was actually faster upwind (with the state of our sails at that time). I enjoyed that series, sailed up to my ability, and managed an even record against *Intrepid* while taking each race from *Valiant* and *Mariner.* The syndicate, however, had expected still more and between the June and July trials filled me with all sorts of advice. Although well intentioned, all this accomplished was to make me nervous. In July, *Intrepid* had a slightly better record. Finally, our sails were perfected to the point that they gave us a slight edge in boat speed by the time the August selection trials commenced. By this time I had been filled with even more advice, was tight as a drum, and was not sailing well.

Because our speed had improved, I managed a four-four record against *Intrepid* in the final trials, while beating *Valiant* and *Mariner* in every race. But I wasn't having any fun at all. I can remember gripping the wheel like a vise. I can recollect pressing my body so hard against the cockpit sides that it hurt. There is absolutely no way you can sail your best in such a frame of mind, and I wasn't. It was small surprise, therefore, that the syndicate kicked me off in favor of Ted Hood, who won the climactic race against *Intrepid* and then went on to sweep *Southern Cross* in the cup match itself. Had I continued to have fun, I am now convinced that I could have sailed *Courageous* to victory, becoming a two-time winner of the America's Cup. By taking myself too seriously, by trying too hard, and by forgetting to have fun, I sailed poorly, considering the level of that competition, and poorly as compared to what I think I was capable of. It was a bitter lesson, but I have only myself to blame.

I hope that the above examples will convince you of the importance of having fun to improve your racing performance. There is, however, an even more important reason. Without fun, sailboat racing simply isn't worthwhile, even if you should manage to win. In this book I have attempted to supply you

How do you picture fun? This is one way Buddy Melges has it. That's him hiking to the extreme while his crew skippers the boat home after winning the Star Worlds.

with a number of keys to racing success. But let's be honest. Most of us don't win except on rare occasions, unless we are competing in an easy class. If you have to win to enjoy yourself, then the sport starts to lose meaning. I deplore what I see as an increasing emphasis in the sport on winning at any cost. Other things being equal, it is more fun to win than to lose and more fun to win in a competitive class than in an easy one. The latter thought prompted me to devote an entire chapter (Chapter 14) to the importance of competing against the best. Doing so is important to enhance your ability and, at the same time, your satisfaction. But if you are not enjoying yourself along the way because of an obsession with winning, it is time to take stock.

Vince Lombardi, the celebrated football coach, is credited with the statement "Winning isn't everything; it's the only thing." That philosophy may or may not work in football, but I simply don't believe it applies to sailboat racing. When winning becomes that important, I feel it is only a matter of time before you stop winning. The stress will get to you. Even if it doesn't and you continue to win, I suspect you will have paid too high a price.

Nor do I buy the dictim "It matters not whether you win or lose; it's how you play the game." It *does* matter, because winning is the apparent goal of competition. Still, this famous quote is perhaps closer to the mark than we might realize, closer than the present trend in the sport. Since most of us will lose more often than we win, the joy must come from the competition itself, from the endeavor to do better, and not just from victory itself. The first two chapters revealed the importance of practice and preparation. Yes, they are important, but you have got to decide for yourself if they are worth the price. There are not too many Dennis Conners willing to devote the better part of two years preparing for a sailboat race, even a race as important as the America's Cup. If you aspire to world-class competition an extreme effort and sacrifice is vital, but *sacrifice* is the key word here. Most of us have a different sense of priorities, or are too lazy to practice or to prepare as hard and as long as we should.

When I was sailing in the International One Design Class, *no one* sailed in practice more than an hour or two a week. It simply didn't occur to us. If any one of the front-runners had spent ten hours each week in practice, I suspect he would have run off from the rest of us. In really tight competition, however, those days are gone forever. Is extreme effort and time worth it for the average sailor, even one sailing in a keen class? For most of us the answer is no.

It is important to realize that by devoting at least a bit more time than you have been in preparation for racing you will do a whole lot better. Beyond that, the law of diminishing returns starts to settle in. Just how much effort and time you are willing to devote is up to you, but even a minor increase will reap handsome dividends.

Championship golfers spend more time practicing than playing. They have to or they won't be champions for long. But I am a hacker and get much more fun out of playing than practicing. Still, with just a bit of practice, I have managed to lower my handicap and improve my scores, with a consequent increase in enjoyment of the sport. If I were younger and more naturally gifted, I might well practice more; but the amount I do now is right for my sense of priorities.

It is a pity that sailing hasn't been able to develop a handicap system (handicapping the sailor's ability rather than the boat's inherent speed, which of course is done). Golf's handicap system allows a less skilled player to compete quite evenly with a fine golfer on a net basis. The good golfer has the pleasure of winning with a lower gross score and the poorer golfer can on any given day win on a net basis after reducing his score by the amount dictated by his handicap. It makes it fun for both, and the hacker can get added fun if he improves and thereby lowers his handicap.

There has developed a schism in sailing between the grand-prix racers and the great bulk of competitive sailors. More power to the grand-prix types who have the time, energy, desire, and *money* to give it a go in the S.O.R.C., the major ocean races, and in the national and world championships in the major one-design classes. But for each sailor of this type, there are at least ten others who simply don't want to compete in such a league. Often, this larger group can get even more competitors to race against in performance-handicap-rating (PHRF) competition or in one-design racing on a local level. And many of the sailors in these classes or events are excellent. Many could excel in the top level of competition if they so elected, but they choose instead to race with family crews or with or against friends. Winning in such competition may not make the headlines, but it can be just as much fun, just as rewarding, and almost as difficult.

It is not too surprising, therefore, that in recent years the major trophy for the Bermuda Race was awarded to the measurement-handicap-system (MHS) winner, as opposed to the winner of the grand-prix I.O.R. division. Neither is it surprising that the low-key cruising race to Bermuda has proved so popular, nor that events such as, in the East, the Off Soundings races or *Yachting* magazine's PHRF Race Week at Block Island and, out West, the Ensenada Race draw such huge fleets, fleets far eclipsing those in the ultracompetitive S.O.R.C. Sailing will remain alive and well just so long as there are events for people to have fun in, without having to make it their career in effort, time, and cash to excel. At the same time, there remains a very real place and purpose for the really major events that can be enjoyed by sailors who are prepared to go all out.

Whether you prefer to sail with another couple or with your family in a local Wednesday evening series, or race with a hot crew in a world championship or major ocean race, you will do better if you have fun. You will have even more fun if you do well and keep improving your skills.

Observing the keys to success in yacht racing will, I am confident, enable you to do better in all levels of competition. This will add to your fun, and that is what the sport is all about.

JOHN HOPF

*I've never been too hot in dinghies, but that's me winning a dinghy series
against all the other 1964 America's Cup contenders. I sailed over my
head because in that year I was having the time of my life and was loose.*

Notes

Notes

Notes

Notes